GooseHead Guide To Life

GooseHead Guide To Life

by Ashley Power

VOLO

HYPERION
NEW YORK

To anyone who has ever had a dream

Special thanks to Elizabeth Lenhard

Printed in the United States of America
First Edition
1 3 5 7 9 10 8 6 4 2
This book is set in11.5/17.5 pt Bookman.
Book designed by Karen Hudson
"Honk" and "Take a Gander @" sidebar spot illustrations by Robert Roper

ISBN 0-7868-1581-7
Visit www.volobooks.com

TaBle oF COnTeNts

I know what you're thinking —

no way did Ashley Power write a book!

This is not an age thing. Plenty of teenage authors have preceded me, from Arthur Rimbaud to Amelia Atwater-Rhodes.

What it is, is a Web thing. Other than the odd sophomore English essay, I'm used to communicating with glowing pixels and streaming video at my Web site, Goosehead.com. I've lived on my iMac and in yours. Plastic, not paper, thank you very much.

For Goosehead fans, seeing my words bound and in print might seem surreal. And for those of you saying, "What the heck is Goosehead.com?" let me explain. . . .

As Internet surfers know it, Goosehead is "The #1 Teen Entertainment Network"—a one-stop shop for chat rooms, bulletin boards, media reviews, no-holds-barred columns, homework help, search engines, and a lot more. It was also the birthplace of my show *Whatever*, which you can now check out on Showtime.

As I know it, Goosehead.com is my hang and my haven. It's a bundle of philosophies. It's a community. It's something I created at age thirteen after pointing, clicking, and sighing my way through a lot of watered-down Web sites for teens. That was a tough year for me, and I was looking for solace on the Web. But I didn't want a fashion catalog, and I didn't want a therapy session. I wanted a place to chill. When I couldn't find an online home sweet home, I made one.

Boy, I did not know what I was getting into.

Boy, I did not know what I was getting into.

In a word, Goosehead has *snowballed.* By the time the site was two years old, we were getting major buzz. My picture was popping up in *Vanity Fair* and *Time*, and Cynthia McFadden from *PrimeTime Live* was jetting out to my home in Burbank, California, to spend a day in the life of a teenage CEO. (And don't think for a minute my friends at school let me live that down. Can you imagine a cameraman following you to your high school football game?!)

Suddenly I was sitting at conference room tables with business experts three times my age, talking profit margins and 80/20 business models. We secured investors and a staff of thirty. Academy Award–winning actor Richard Dreyfuss signed on as an artistic adviser and all-around, mustachioed cheerleader. And feminist drag-racer icon Shirley Muldowney drove a cool hot-pink car in the NHRA U.S. Nationals with our lopsided logo—Goosehead.com—painted on the hood.

It's been an extraordinary time. Am I an extraordinary teenager? I would say that I'm idealistic. It never occurred to me that a thirteen-year-old's home page couldn't eventually get a hundred thousand hits a day. I never dreamed that the lack of a driver's license meant I couldn't be a

CEO. I have plenty of opinions—and nobody ever gave me a good reason to keep them bottled up. And when I got an opportunity to branch out from my usual medium—the Web—again I said, "Why not?" That's why I've written this book.

What will you find here? There's plenty about my personal history, about growing up in a way nontraditional family and suffering through the emotional traumas that litter teenage life like land mines. You'll also hear just what life as a teenage dot.com CEO is like, and you'll learn how to become a Web maven yourself.

And what about advice? *Life's Little Rulebook*, by Ashley Power?

Well, just as Goosehead.com isn't your typical teen scene, the *Goosehead Guide to Life* is not one of those books that's going to tell you what to do. I trust you can figure that out yourself. But I will tell you what I've done in the different situations life has thrown at me. I'll share my thoughts on issues that affect and intrigue me, from navigating the dating scene to staging the perfect Girls' Night In, from avoiding drugs to dealing with the deaths of loved ones.

I don't care to teach a class called Teen Life 101, but I do have a mission—I want to provide some tools and a little inspiration to teens who want to make their voices heard. Maybe after reading my story, you'll launch your own Web site (hey, Goosehead welcomes competition). Flash ain't your thing? Write an e-zine, a political leaflet, a chain letter, a rally cry . . . whatever.

A word about that word—*whatever*. Parents hate it, right? *Whatever* is the mantra of our generation. Some people think of it as a verbal shrug of the shoulders, an *um* or *uh* or other meaningless way to take up space.

I *so* beg to differ.

As my character Skye Warner says at the beginning of our show, "*Whatever* means a number of things. It means, okay, you can do whatever you want." My American Heritage dictionary defines *whatever* as "everything and anything."

Exactly.

Our potential—mine, yours, Goosehead.com's—is everything and anything. If there's anything I hope you'll take away from the riffs and musings in this guide to life, it's that idea, that anything's possible.

PART I:

All About Ashley

Photos from top to bottom: my first flower girl experience—
I am 2 ½ years old; 9 years old, February 11, 1995;
me at 6 months old

I'm 2 weeks old!

Chapter One History 101

Life is full of little surprises. And I was one of them. At eighteen, my mom didn't expect to have a baby. But there was no stopping me. I guess I always had a head start.

In the Beginning

My mom and dad met in high school, dated, and were married October 19, 1984, in La Mirada, California. I arrived seven months later on May 9, 1985. During my first few years I grew very close to my mother. She had custody of me after my parents' divorce when I was a baby.

Extended Family . . .

I couldn't have been more loved as a kid. I think the fact that my mom was so young made her a more conscientious mother. She always worries she's not a good mom. Not only has she been the best mom, she's one of my best friends. I really love my family and feel so blessed.

My grandmother was and is totally doting. When my mom acted like, well, a mom, doing that discipline thing, I would run crying to Grandma.

"Mommy's so mean!" I'd declare.

"Oh, she is!" my grandmother would agree. Way to encourage a wayward child, Grandma! :-)

My mother's best friend, Kelly, was like a big sister to me. She knew just what it took to make a little kid happy—lots of girlie accessories and cute shoes. (My mom can thank Kelly for creating my lasting obsession with cool footwear.)

And then there was my baby-sitter, Margie Simon, who also baby-sat my mom when she was a kid. To us kids, she's Nina. Nina is from Luxembourg, and she has an accent I've never been able to imitate. When I was born, she was at the hospital, and after that, I became a regular at her chaotic, home-based day care. Often my mom would cart me over there in the mornings when I was still asleep. I'd arise a few hours later, totally unfreaked to be waking up in a strange bed. Then I'd join a wild pack of kids in the backyard for all-day play. Nina's house was my house.

My mom and dad at their high school prom

The fact that she usually refused to take money for her baby-sitting services made her all the more like a second mom.

But eventually, I came to have an actual second mom, of sorts. My dad married my stepmother, Melanie, when I was five or six. He also adopted Melanie's two young kids, Whitney and Zach. So, for a few weeks out of each year, I got to slip into big-sister mode in a family of five.

A Girl of Independent Means

Even with the support of many, those early years were still tough. Mom was working nights and putting herself through college during the days. And when she wasn't working, she was tired!

I learned to entertain myself from the get-go. A lot of mornings, I'd wake up and toddle out to the kitchen by myself. I'd climb onto the counter to get my cereal bowl and

Every blade of grass has its angel that bends over it and whispers, "Grow, grow."
—The Talmud

GolDeN Egg

pour myself some breakfast. Then I'd pop in a Disney video (of course, I'd learned to work the VCR when I was two) and munch my breakfast with *The Little Mermaid* until my mom got up.

Then we'd go to college.

Yup, I was one highly educated kid. I went to a ton of lectures with my mom. She'd take notes while I sat on the floor and played quietly. If I'd listened up a bit, I could have aced the AP exams in kindergarten! Alas . . . I was more interested in my crayons and coloring books than Psych 101.

One thing I did learn at college, though, was how to negotiate the weird world of adults. I think that as young children, we have this ability to

August 1987. My mom's twenty-first
birthday. I am two.

learn in any environment. I was learning how to deal with adults, for better or worse. While some kids spent all their time in the sheltered kiddie land of day care and play dates, I did a lot of hanging with my mom and her friends. Grown-ups were just really tall pals to me.

Today I realize that those were the years that helped shape me and my ability to run Goosehead. I learned to be independent—fiercely so. I loved doing things on my own, which is exactly what I had to do as a young up-and-coming CEO.

"WHATEVER"

You Know You're Wiser Than Your Years When . . .

- Your dad asks your permission to marry his new wife.
- Your mom says, "You know, I have my period and I'm not in a good mood," and you have to tell her, "Ma, I'm in second grade. I don't know what the heck a period is." Whereupon she sits down and explains to you not just the basic birds and bees, but all the subtleties of those special Midol moments.
- You lose your two front teeth at the tender age of three. The whole story? I fell and my teeth ended up turning a sick brown—they were DOA. So, I was carted to the dentist to have them pulled, and man, was I pissed. In the waiting room, they tried to appease us kids with a *Sleeping Beauty* video, but I wasn't fooled. *This is ridiculous!* I remember thinking. *They're going to hurt us all, but they're trying to make us think that they're nice people.*

And I was down with grown-ups. This was another necessity for the future, when I'd be working with adults as my equal or my employees at Goosehead, Inc.

Without my grown-up-centric childhood, who knows if I would have had what it takes to become a dot.com mogul? (I use that term *mogul* loosely.)

Money, Money

My mom and me at my kindergarten graduation

I also learned about adult concerns like money pretty early. Money was one of the reasons that, at age six, I spent eight months living with my dad and his new family in Utah.

My mom had graduated from college that year. You think a college degree guarantees that you land on your feet? Not even. Between school loans and our living expenses, Mom had a pile of debt to pay off.

She had to make a choice—start her career with a nine-to-five job or make twice as much money waiting tables at a bar from four in the afternoon until 3 A.M. every night. Putting off her career for a few months meant Mom could get us on financial track more quickly.

It also meant she had almost no time to take care of me.

So I went to stay with Dad for the school year. My mom said it almost killed her to see me go, but it was the best option for me at the time.

The irony is, when I got to Utah, the money sitch was even tighter.

My dad was working as a car salesman, and he was also tithing—a custom in which a family donates ten percent of their annual income to the Mormon church. Melanie, my stepmom, stayed home with us kids full-time.

Between tithing and supporting the family, my dad found himself one day with nothing but seven dollars in his pocket. We were broke.

But if there's anything you can say about Dad, it's that he has a lot of faith in life. There he was with nothing but a few crumpled bills in his pocket, and he said, "You know what? Let's have fun. Let's enjoy this night."

So we went to Arby's and bought seven dollars' worth of french fries and went home. We poured them into a bowl and each got our own plate for ketchup. Then we pigged out and had a blast. At the time, my siblings and I didn't understand what dire straits we were in. To us, it was a party.

And here's the freaky thing. The next day, $500 my dad hadn't been expecting arrived in our hands. It was enough to tide us over. We were broke no more.

Now, every once in a while when I get together with Dad, Melanie, Whitney, and Zach, we have "French fry parties" just like that first one. Mostly it's goofy and nostalgic, but it also gives me the slightest case of the chills— reminding me just how precarious things were back then.

If there's anything I learned from those days—it's that independence and financial savvy are vital. To this day, I know that my family will take care of me. But it gives me peace of mind to know that I've learned a thing or two about standing on my own two feet.

The ever-growing Power family: Dad, Isabelle, Calvin, Elliot, Zack, me, Whitney, and Melanie

The Family Grows

The Family Grows

When I was five, my mother started dating my soon-to-be stepdad, Mark Schilder. The thing about Mark is, he's one of those people who excels at almost anything he tries. It's really amazing and also extremely frustrating. Sometimes, when you're around him you feel like a total loser because you can't do everything he can do. Graphic design, painting, writing, directing, photography—you name it, Mark can do it. As I said, frustrating. Okay, probably just some jealousy on my side, but hey, I'm just a teenager. By the way, I'm a much better dancer than he is. Which really means that he can't dance at all, since I can barely find rhythm in a song.

Mom and Mark's wedding day

He quickly became a constant in our lives, but at first, I didn't like him at all! He had a sarcastic sense of humor that I just didn't get. He would tease me when I sang along to songs on the radio (and didn't know the words), and he loved to rub my face in it if he beat me at a game. Example, he took me to play miniature golf when I was five years old. On one of the holes (I think it was the windmill one), my ball ended up right against the cement railing, and I went to move it. He was like totally yelling, "You can't do that—it's against the rules!" Yep, against the rules, very true. Are you kidding me? (I love you, Mark, but let's be honest—I was only five!) Today I'd be totally amused and do the same thing to him, but back then, I would burst into tears.

13

I can't say exactly what brought me around to being best friends with Mark. I think we just found a common ground to stand on. I knew Mark raged in front of the mirror—doing that rock-star-fantasy thing—just like I did. We both loved the same movies. And I never got tired of hearing his stories about ex-girlfriends and hanging out with celebrities that he knew.

Mark's opinion came to matter to me, too—whether he was commenting on a drawing I'd made or an outfit I was wearing. I'd crave that recognition and approval that made me feel pretty or something to be proud of. Mark is one of the few people who can make me feel good when everyone else has failed.

That's why I remember being totally psyched when I came home from school one afternoon in 1994 to find Mark, pacing the family room nervously.

"When your mother gets home," he told me, "I'm going to ask her to marry me."

We waited for her together. And true to his word, Mark promptly popped the question the minute Mom walked through the door.

Four years later, life changed a lot more for all of us. Enter my baby brother, Joshua Sloan Schilder.

Josh, who is now three, is a little tow-headed terror (and I

Josh and me, 1998. I am in eighth grade.

mean that in the most loving way, of course). He's majorly into everything and always giggling.

There were times when he was an infant that I couldn't help resenting him a little. Josh's entrée into our household meant my parents were home a lot more, but with less time to give me. I had less time to myself to just sing and dance around my room and be goofy or gloomy in peace. I also had to do my share of baby-sitting. And when friends came over, we were constantly being shushed. "The baby's sleeping!"

Mark and me, Las Vegas, April 2000

When Josh became a toddler, our house became Grand Central Station for every little kid on our block. Imagine being out on a Friday night until two, only to be awakened at nine the next morning by a pack of squealing kids watching *Barney*. Not funny.

But it is funny how quickly Josh became a fixture in our family. I can barely remember what it was like before he existed. And I can't wait for him to grow a little older so we can have five-year-old heart-to-hearts and I can start giving him advice about negotiating the cutthroat world of kindergarten.

 Take a Gander @

My **little brother's** site! Wild man Josh!
www.goosehead.com/goosevillage/GooseRoad/josh

My dad's family moved from Utah to Missouri and was also growing. In addition to Whitney and Zach, Melanie and my dad have had three children together.

I've never lived with Elliot, Calvin, and Isabelle the way I did with Zach and Whitney when I was six, but Dad always gives me the day-to-day updates on their lives. To them I'm their very big sister who lives very far away. As my dad's first kid, sometimes I feel lost in the shuffle of the big, chaotic Power household.

It's hard at times going from my California home, where I have my own room with a door I can shut, to Missouri, where I share a room and there's always someone wanting to play.

But as someone who was an only child for much of her life, it's also a trip doing that Big Family thing every once in a while.

Welcome to Hollywood

In Burbank, half the people you meet seem to be child actors, tromping to commercial auditions and head-shot shoots the way kids in the rest of the country go to soccer practice or piano lessons. It's no big thing.

Okay, so here's where it gets out of hand and how I got the showbiz bug. Mark's best friend, Doug McKeon, was getting married. He's an actor, and we all went to the wedding. I think I was about nine years old. After the wedding, when we were going to the reception, there were three limousines, and I had never ridden in one, and I really wanted to. So, my mom said it was okay, and off I went. What my parents didn't know at the time was that in the car were agents and managers.

It only took eleven miles for me to decide that I wanted to be an actress. The car came to a stop at the reception; I exited and announced, "I want to be an actress!" I remember the look on Mark's face as he walked over to the car, looked inside, and announced, "Who do I have to thank for this?" For my parents, it was like the last thing they wanted. But they said if I wanted to try acting, I could, and that's how that started. One of the people in that limo (Mel McKeon) became my manager, and off I went. With no idea what I was getting into.

Take one of my biggest commercial gigs, for French Toast Crunch cereal. I got a callback (as in, audition number two) for the commercial while I was at sleep-away camp, several hours from home. Since it was a national commercial and big-time gig, my mom drove all the way up to pick me up and take me to the reading, where I was competing against a boy (the casting director's first choice).

My dog Buddy, posing for a photo with me. I'm nine years old.

So there I was at this studio, scratching my mosquito bites and sitting in front of a committee of commercial honchos. Of course, the first thing I did was spill my picturesque bowl of French Toast Crunch all over the floor!

I ad-libbed through it, belting out a big, cute "Oops! Dropped my French Toast Crunch!" Ugh. The next day, I was back at camp, writing off the whole thing.

But unbelievably, I got the gig. That was the first time I learned that there's no predicting your success in Hollywood. When you think you've tanked, you get the job. When you ace the audition, they'll be all "Oh, we decided we want a green-eyed brunette."

My biggest acting job was a starring role in a movie called *The Secret Agent Club*. I was ten years old, and the cast was full of other kids — filming was a blast. But the truth is, the acting part of the job didn't excite me nearly as much as watching the film's director, John Murlowski, at work.

I hounded him with questions and watched as he gave orders to the crew. He let me peek through the camera while he set up shots, and I listened in on all the advice he gave the actors.

And I immediately revised my future plans. Acting was great and everything, but what I really wanted to do was direct. Besides, I hated auditioning, and I didn't really care about being a star. I think that you really need to have that attitude if you are going to make it as an actor. You have to want it really bad. You have to want to be a star. When I hear people say, "I just want to act. I don't care about being famous," I think, That's a lie. Some part of you has to want the spotlight.

Part of the reason I launched *Whatever* on Goosehead.com was because I had visions of opening credits that said, "Written, directed, and produced by Ashley Power." When it came down to it, though, I realized I

GolDeN Egg

Our deepest fear is not that we are inadequate. Our deepest fear is that we are powerful beyond measure. We ask ourselves, who am I to be brilliant, gorgeous, talented, and fabulous? Actually, who are you not to be? You are a child of God. Your playing small doesn't serve the world. There's nothing enlightened about shrinking so that other people won't feel insecure around you. We were born to make manifest the glory of God that is within us. It's not just in some of us, it's in everyone. And as we let our own light shine, we unconsciously give other people permission to do the same. As we are liberated from our own fear, our presence automatically liberates others.

—Marianne Williamson

wasn't quite ready to helm an entire series, and I settled into cowriting scripts with Mark and playing Skye Warner in the show. Which at first I thought, "That's not really what I want to do." But Mark said, "Who understands this character better than you? You wrote it. You are her. You should play the part."

But I'm still watching and learning. Directing, I have a hunch, is just around the corner.

A Budding Web Mogul Is Born

I was one of the first kids on the block to have her own computer. I was eight years old, and it was the cutest little Mac. I loved it. I used it to sloooowly type up reports for school, and I also fiddled around a lot with a program called Creative Writer, which taught you how to write stories, create pictures, and design your own little-kid publications.

When I was nine, Mark called me into the living room, where we kept our big family computer. He showed me this really cool new thing called AOL. And wouldn't you know, the very first thing I logged into was a teen chat. Mark taught me how the conversation worked. I was fascinated and immediately signed up for an e-mail address. At this point, most of my buds had never even heard of AOL! But it didn't take long for me to drag them onto the bandwagon.

By the next year, I was so interested in all things pixelated that I took a summer Photoshop course at a nearby high school. By then, I was living on my Mac. I IM-ed friends all the time, chatted, e-mailed, and did tons of research on the Web. Logging on had become routine for me.

In hindsight, I realize I was preparing to be a Webmaster long before the desire to be one ever crossed my mind. As I spearheaded Web use among my friends, taught myself everything I could about the Internet, and delved deeper into the wonders of my little Mac, I was putting myself on a total trajectory toward Goosehead.com. It would just take a few years for me to realize it.

Kind of makes you believe in fate, doesn't it?

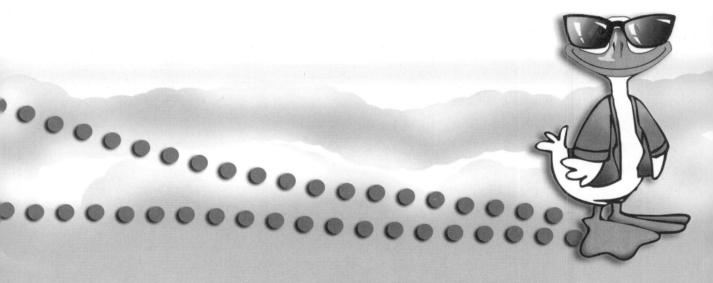

Chapter Two
The Birth of Goosehead.com

The Back Story . . .

As a little kid, I used the Internet mostly for research. But in my thirteenth year, I started looking for more from the Web. I wanted . . . a little bit of everything: Information. Chats. Cool things to see. Fun things to do. A hangout.

I suppose those were out there somewhere. So what was missing? A voice. I wanted to know that someone real—someone I could relate to—was posting all this stuff. And I didn't want adults telling me what they thought was cool.

So there I was, trying not so successfully to click away my boredom, when something awful happened. My eighth-grade class was scheduled to go on a weeklong trip—seven days of sunning, traveling, and hanging out instead of sitting in class. So what was wrong with that, you ask?

Well, it's a long story. . . .

I've switched schools a lot in my sixteen years, but no move was more life changing than my fateful shift from seventh to eighth grade. My seventh-grade class at St. Michael's and All Angels was beyond small—we're talking eighteen students. In those years at my cozy little school, I came into my own. I became comfortable with who I was and totally independent. So much so that—as the year came to an end—I felt the need to spread out and meet new people. I decided to switch to a new school with a larger student body. It was hard leaving my small, safe environment and becoming the "new kid" (again!). Looking back, I'm glad I went through with it, because I learned so much about myself and about life.

But at the time, it was really difficult.

Now, this is a touchy subject because eighth grade wasn't that long ago—many of my classmates are still in my world. So, let's leave the details in my diary and just say I had a bit of a run-in with a group of people that year. You know the story: one day I was making new friends and learning the lay of the land, the next I was getting prank phone calls and people were spreading rumors about me.

Naturally, this phenom left me totally confused and majorly upset. I know I am not perfect. I mess up all the time. But still I could never put my finger on anything I did that would have caused all that trouble. I just wanted to get along with everyone.

In fact, I can't remember exactly how my yearlong fight with

GolDeN Egg

I think we all have the power to shine in our own ways. But you know that tired old saying, "No man is an island?" It's true. I think we shine even brighter when we share our lives and wisdom with others. Not only do you show that person that he or she is important, but you can reflect their light, too.

those kids began. And you know what? It probably didn't matter much at the time, either. I was that year's black sheep, and that's all there was to it.

Of course, I wasn't on the outs with everyone. I want to say thank you to those few people in my grade and the grades above who helped me get through that year. Even if I don't talk to all of them any longer, they will never be forgotten: Ashley, Daniella, Jake, Gillian, Sydney, Courtni, and Derrick, to name a few.

My thirteenth birthday

But even with this support, I felt like a loser at school. I had only a couple of friends and ate lunch alone a lot. I wasn't very busy on the weekends, either. Sometimes after a particularly rough day at school, say someone had winged a glob of food at me in the cafeteria or planned some other small but searing humiliation—it was all I could do not to burst into tears in the hall. But that was one of my triumphs that year—I never let them see me cry. Sure, as soon as I shut my mom's car door for the ride home from school, those tears flowed like there was no tomorrow. But the kids at school had no idea.

I knew I had to have faith and not beat up on myself. I can only be me and if people don't like that, they're not worth my time. It's easier said than done, I know.

How can you keep walking when people are staring at you, whispering behind your back, laughing, throwing things at you, telling lies, and calling you names? Well, I focused on my schoolwork and wrote. I played basketball. I did anything I could do to keep my mind off junior-high politics.

I learned to just keep walking at school. I realized that the things certain classmates said about me weren't true and I knew deep down in my heart who I was. I wasn't going to let them define me. I ignored it. I also started surfing the Web more, seeking refuge in an e-community where nobody knew that I was a fourteen-year-old pariah.

It's funny, now that I'm a couple years away from eighth grade, I look back at those times—when I thought life itself would END—and laugh. I also feel lucky, believe it or not. We grow from every experience no matter how painful, and that year I had plenty of 'em. Without all that stuff in my history, perhaps I wouldn't have what it takes to run Goosehead.com, or to write this book.

I remember a warm sunny day last summer when I sat down with my friend Mike. (Mike was the one who first introduced me to Papa Roach, something I'll always owe him for!) We were talking about life and I mentioned I was thinking about writing a book. The idea made me nervous, to say the least. I'd never written a book before. It's not something the average high-school girl does. But Mike reassured me.

"Look at what you've gone through, Ash," he said. "There are so many people out there who've gone through the same stuff, or who've felt the way you did. It would help them to read about your experiences."

I think Mike was right. We all go through times in life where we feel so alone. It helps to know that someone understands; has run a tough gauntlet and come out okay. That's why I'm not using these pages to tell everyone how perfect and easy my life has been. Because it wasn't, it isn't, and never will be.

"That which does not kill us makes us stronger," right?

Which brings me back to that empty week, when my entire eighth-grade class was going on a field trip and I was staying home. There I was with a week of white space—no homework, no transportation, no nothing, not even a perfect place to roost on the Web.

So I created one.

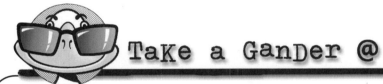 TaKe a GanDer @

Letters to a Young Poet, by Rainer Maria Rilke

This collection of letters between a writer and a student covers so much more than verse. The writer sends the young man letters about love and growing and learning—about life itself. "Do not complain to life," he writes, for instance, "complain to yourself." One of my favorite quotes is "Pretend you are the very first man and then write what you see and experience what you love and lose." I have read and reread this book many times and still get something new out of it every time. *Letters to a Young Poet* is inspiring and reminds me that I am a part of something bigger than the problems that go on in my house or my high school.

Goosehead.com

Goosehead.com

Have I mentioned my stubborn streak? Well, once I decided that I could do better than all the teen sites floating around the Web, I was on a tear.

It started as an innocent little home page. Make that a filled-with-glitches, Web-naive little home page. I was a newbie through and through. *HTML for Dummies* was glued to my desk and still, my first attempts were pretty bad. I sucked at hand coding.

But I knew what I liked. So, instead of wasting time being jealous when I happened upon a bitchin' Java script or a cool graphic, I contacted the Webmaster himself. (Yes, it was usually a he. We femme masters are still outnumbered.)

Through my e-mail correspondence, I learned to read source code. I filled my site with new Java scripts. I learned about the wonders of Photoshop and began to wrap my brain around design.

And then I told all my friends. At this point, my home page was simply a place for me and my buds to hang.

The name, you ask? Though it would seem easy enough, trying to name my home page was like naming a baby. I was paralyzed. Nothing came to mind except, for some reason, a silly cement goose in the front yard of my house.

Decapitated goose ornament

This goose came to a sorry end on the day we moved in 1997. I was carrying boxes inside, and I wasn't watching where I was going. So naturally, I tripped over the stupid goose. I was merely injured, but the goose was a goner—decapitated. Perhaps it was guilt that made me name my site Goosehead.com. Maybe it was just creative desperation. Anyway, the name stuck.

And so did the site. Word was getting out, which I guess is why they call it the World Wide Web. People who didn't even know me were clicking

This was my first Goosehead Web site. I was still learning.

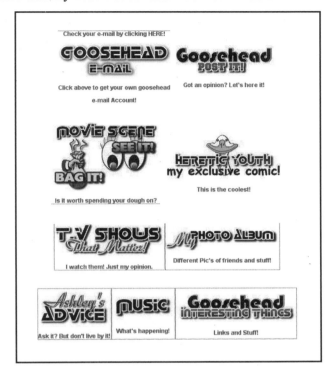

in to check out my hangout, which was becoming increasingly buff as my design skills and tech savvy got stronger.

Pretty soon, I'd wangled my way up the ladder at certain choice search engines. That meant when one typed *teen* into the engine, Goosehead might pop up in the first ten suggestions, instead of eight screen loads down.

It wasn't long before I was getting forty thousand hits a day.

But was I satisfied? Noooooo.

Not when I heard about this fabulous new thing called Broadband.

CyberSafety . . .

I don't want to sound like your parents and bombard you with rules and regulations in regard to chatting or surfing the Web. Mainly because when my parents warned me, I don't think I was listening very well and learned (after being yelled at later) that you have to be smart when you're on the Internet. Don't give out too much info about yourself and it's never a good idea to make plans to meet an AOL friend or e-mail buddy no matter how tempting it may be. You have to take care of yourself, and in doing that, you never want to put yourself in a vulnerable position.

Act One, Scene One

Act One, Scene One

By now, RealPlayer and the like are so 1999, but back at the start of Goosehead.com, streaming media felt like buried treasure. It felt like every aspiring filmmaker with a mouse could whip up a movie and instantly distribute it on the Web.

But one movie wasn't enough for me. I was thinking . . . series.

That's when I knew I had to consult my parents. I live within walking distance of half a dozen film studios. So I knew that prime time required dollars, and a lot of them.

I gulped down my fear and informed my parents that I'd been doing a little . . . *outreach* for my home page. It took a few minutes for the reality to hit Mark—I'd become e-pen pals with dozens of strangers. Grown-ups. Hackers. Men.

Okay, so after he hit the roof? Mark was really impressed. And after he gave Goosehead a good, hard look, he also knew I had something there. So, he started working the phones. When it was clear that my contacts were ordinary computer geeks with honorable intentions, he arranged for us all to meet in Las Vegas. To tell you the truth, I don't think Mark was totally convinced at this point that Goosehead would work. So, he figured, why not go to Vegas? Where the adults could gamble if all else failed. Looking back on it, they all took a bigger gamble than any of them I think ever expected.

And that's how I found myself in a hotel conference room "taking a meeting." I was dry-mouthed and totally intimidated but trying to play it cool as I convinced a bunch of adults that they should support this endeavor of mine. Luckily they all seemed to agree with my ideas and helped finance Goosehead as we took it to the next level of Webdom. Everyone supported the idea of Broadband shows, *Whatever* being the first one, a comedy series about the real life of teenagers—nose picking, swear words, lying to parents, zits and all.

After we expanded Goosehead and launched *Whatever*, reporters started to flock to my house like sixth graders to an 'NSYNC concert. It turns out a fifteen-year-old girl CEO is a bit of an oddity, even in these equal-opportunity Webby times. Posing for photographers for hours at a time and listening to reporters ask me the same questions again and again is not why I got into this business. But doing all that publicity got Goosehead more exposure and, most important, more teenagers scrolling through our pages. So it was worth it.

It also helped us make a deal for a two hour pilot that's going to take *Whatever* from the tiny screen that is RealPlayer and QuickTime to the small screen that is TV.

Life as CEO . . .

As surreal as it can sometimes be seeing "Ashley Power, CEO" on my letterhead, mostly that title feels pretty natural to me. I think running Goosehead or a company in general is what I was always meant to do.

If you gave me one of those silly "Test Your Personality" quizzes, it would probably tell me to run, don't walk, to the nearest Young Democrats club meeting. Leadership is in my blood. That's why I prefer directing to acting, solitude to running with cliques, and DIY to delegating.

Of course, as Goosehead has grown, I've realized delegating is the only way I'm going to have a life. There's way too much for one person to do now: publicity and promotion, selling advertising, making deals with investors, keeping the site up and humming, designing new Goosehead pages, courting alliances with other teen sites, building our own search engine . . . whew! These are only a handful of my responsibilities.

So, at this point, there are a bunch of people, from my parents and grandmother to our Goosehead office staff to our many adjunct helper elves, who make that stuff happen while I'm biding my time in algebra class. (Believe me, that can be agonizing! I've been known to duck into the girls' room at school to call the office and check on things.)

So, What Do I Do as a CEO?

Not a typical CEO type, huh?

Well, if they had a CEO school, they'd tell you that you are the "big picture" person. Since I can no longer attend to the details of putting Goosehead together, I focus on the site's overall direction. Recently, for instance, I added a makeup and fashion page and hired my friend Kristin to write for it.

I also cowrite scripts for *Whatever* and help develop other shows. I do face time on the Goosehead chat. I respond to e-mails asking for advice.

And I also take a lot of meetings. Meetings, meetings, and yes, more meetings! Meetings with studio heads interested in developing *Whatever* and other Goosehead TV ideas, meetings with investors and artistic advisers like Richard Dreyfuss, meetings with celebrities I interview on the site, meetings with my staff so I can communicate what I've picked up in all the other meetings! Well . . . you get the idea.

It seems like heady stuff. But overall, my life is not that different from that of any teenager with a really consuming job. I could be flipping burgers or working at a movie theater. I just happened to have created my own job. Like anything else in life—be it adjusting to a new family member or adjusting to your freshman year in high school—doing all things Goosehead has become pretty normal to me.

I don't prance around my house, telling my parents, "I'm the boss of you." Not if I want to live to be seventeen. No, they're still very much the boss of me, thank you.

Even though I'm a CEO, I still do homework!

I don't answer my home phone with, "Ashley Power, may I help you?" No, it's just, "Hey."

I don't cringe and quaver when I'm working with adults. I act like I have a right to be there. After all, I need these adults' connections and expertise, but they need my teenage input. And we all have a common goal—to make Goosehead the best that it can be.

I try, as much as possible, to keep life at school normal and low-key. I don't usually advertise my TV and magazine appearances because (a) that's dorky and (b) some people respond with bitterness and jealousy. Not that there's really anything glamorous about photo shoots—once you've been through one, you've been through them all. Brush the hair, curl the hair, makeup, wardrobe, pink top, blue top, red pants, black pants, outside, inside, stand, kneel, sit, stand again, chin down, eyes up, change clothes, more lipstick, turn your head, smile! Trust me, you're not missin' much.

And then after posing, you play the waiting game, wondering which picture the magazine will choose.

You would think doing the CEO thing would make me more serious. After all, I've got a lot of pressure on my shoulders. My parents and partners have invested their hard-earned cash in Goosehead, and now people's jobs are riding on the site, too. Eek!

The thing is, I don't think running Goosehead has turned me into a stodgy, boss-man type. If anything, its success has made me more creative, more open to anything and everything, whether it's coming up with a rad idea for the site or making a ballsy connection at a Britney Spears party. (That's where I met the singer T. J. Espinoza, who later joined Goosehead's staff.)

In fact, I think the most valuable asset I have under my belt is the same one you all have—youth. Without it, maybe half the crazy/brilliant ideas that have made Goosehead what it is would never have seen the light of day.

Some people don't think we curfew-ditching, attitudinal teens are responsible enough to ever accomplish something really major like Goosehead.com. And guess what? They're wrong. If I can do it, anyone can!

"WHATEVER"

Not every photo shoot makes me look like a glamour girl. Take *CosmoGIRL!*, for example. Frequently asked question . . . "What was up with that picture in *CosmoGIRL!* magazine?!"

The answer? I spent the day in New York with this photographer taking really artsy, edgy, bitchin' photos only to open the magazine to see my eyes bug out of my head in a not-so-cute picture. That alone makes you not excited to jump in front of that camera once more.

But they're just pictures; it's just a photo shoot. Some will be good, and some will be bad. No one is perfect, and even though I wasn't overjoyed to see my head pop off the page, it doesn't keep me up at night.

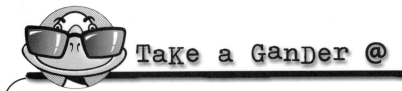

Hawk, Occupation: Skateboarder by Tony Hawk, with Sean Mortimer.

Tony Hawk, in large part, made skating what it is today—X-Games, milk ads, and all. He pioneered the sport by following his passions, not pop culture. Tony's a total inspiration to me, a reminder to always, always push your limits, ignore the naysayers, and work it. Plus, his book made me laugh out loud.

PART II:

The World According to Ashley

Photos from top to bottom: my first prom; my drawing of my mom and me. I win second place in an art contest; publicity photo

Chatting on the phone in my home "office"

Chapter Three
Friendship

I've heard a time will come when I don't feel the need to spend every free moment with a phone glued to my ear. Frankly, I find this hard to believe. I'm sixteen—my friends are my life. But as you well know, life at sixteen is fraught with drama, as well as fun.

Think of all the changes that happen in that transition from the tweens to the teens. You discover the opposite sex, your body changes (in my case, I put on weight—oh, joy!), you learn to drive, you start fighting with your parents. . . . The list goes on and on.

Relationships change as well. I know they do for me as I sort my way through my personal growth, deciding what I really want and need in my life.

Six Degrees of Friendship

Six Degrees of Friendship

If every one of my friends was a "best friend," I'd not only be overextended, I'd be lying. In truth, I have a lot of different friends in my life.

Take my childhood pal, Arelyn. We became best buds in third grade. We did all the third-grade stuff together—sleep-overs, "Greased Lightning" in the living room, giggling nonstop. But in fifth grade, Arelyn moved to Sacramento and later, Rhode Island.

Our friendship didn't end, but it changed. We didn't talk every day or even every week. We called each other once in a blue moon, and if we were lucky, we got to visit once or twice a year. But somehow, whenever I did talk to Arelyn, we'd just pick up where we left off. Now that Arelyn's back in California, we still don't see each other as much as we'd like (though it's easier now that I have a driver's license), yet every time I see her, I am beyond comfortable. I know she will be a friend for the rest of my life.

Blessed is the influence of one true loving human soul on another.
—George Eliot

GolDeN Egg

I guess that's because we have a shared history. She remembers me when I was a goofy eight-year-old in "Limited Too" outfits. She'll never get sick of teasing me about Cammeron, the guy I was madly in love with from third to fifth grade.

New friends can be glamorous—like new . . . anything. But nothing replaces history. And no matter how distant Arelyn and I are in miles, we'll always have that.

Lindsay, who I met six years ago, feels like a sister. Fights, tears, slamming doors all included. She's the type of friend you fight with but at the end of the day you still love. We're so different that I think we balance each other out sometimes.

Goosehead has expanded my circle of friends a great deal. I have colleagues at the office, e-mail buds, chat mates, and a lot of professional associations that are totally casual and fun.

I also have several friends who are in their late teens and early twenties. They're in college or just getting started in the working world. Some are trying to make it as actors in Hollywood and struggling to pay the bills. Others are dealing with the angst of leaving home for the first time, shouldering grown-up responsibilities or going through their first serious relationships.

I love having these older friends who, like me, work in the real world. Talking to them about work stresses gives me perspective on, say, getting detention at school for wearing an out-of-uniform sweater or stressing about my date (or lack of one!) for homecoming.

Bottom line? It would be safe, but boring, if all my friends were just like me. I like a little diversity in my friend pool.

You've Got Mail

A while ago, I got an e-mail at Goosehead.com from Ella Hooper, a seventeen-year-old Australian girl in the band Killing Heidi. We e-mailed back and forth, and then we started talking on the phone. She told me about her band and sent me a CD. I had no idea that Killing Heidi was such a huge success in Australia—she never told me that. We just talked about how much we liked music and how much we both had in common with each other.

When Ella came to L.A., we made plans to meet. It's weird when you meet someone in person, even though you've talked to him or her a bunch on the phone. You think, what if we don't like each other? But we clicked. Although we look so opposite walking down the street (she has black dreads with ever-changing color extensions, and I have sun-streaked blond hair), we happen to be very much alike. While I am in and out of meetings, she is keeping up a busy tour schedule. We both have businesses that we need to manage. But whenever we meet, we have a blast hanging out together. Shopping is always on the agenda, but so is talking about Web sites, boys, family, and business. It's funny, we've known each other for less than a year, but she has become a really important friend to me.

The guys in the band are great, too. Jesse Hooper, Adam Pedretti, and Warren (known as "Waz" or "Wazza") are very cool. Jesse always laughs at me when I complain that his chords are too hard. And Adam and Waz have generously made me feel a part of the Killing Heidi family.

Ella is the only person who doesn't mind when I call her at 2 A.M. L.A. time—of course, it is already 9 P.M. Australia time! But Ella is a true friend and always listens to me—and I try to be there for her, too. She writes all her own lyrics and shares so much of her life through her music. She will always have a place in my heart.

And it all started with an e-mail. . . .

The Opposite Sex
The Opposite Sex

And let's not forget the all-important friends of the opposite sex. I love the platonic relationships I have with my male friends. It's such a relief to get inside the foreign land that is a guy's head without having romantic feelings complicate things. Not to say that complication never occurs; I've been on both sides of the Dawson–Joey syndrome.

But I enjoy my guy friends' company because I know there's never any competition. Girls can sometimes be catty or jealous, but I know my boy bud isn't trying to snag my new pink tank-top style, so there are no worries.

Guy friends are also great allies on the dating front. Your friend might be able to clear up some mystery of the male or female mating behavior. (Don't count on it, though. A lot of my guy friends explain bad behavior to me this way: "I dunno, Ash. We're just stupid!")

Or say you have a crush. Your friend can do a little reconnaissance work and find out if the feelings go both ways. (That is, if you're willing to do the same for him or her!) S/he can also give you inside information on your crush. This is especially important if the person in question has a reputation for treating significant others badly.

Who's That in the Mirror?

GolDeN Egg

A lot of souls have been lost to the cause of "fitting in." In trying to be who the cool kids want you to be, it's easy to lose sight of who you are.

I may be fairly independent, but I haven't always been immune to the urge to merge.

I'd be in the car with some friends when a song came on the radio.

"Oh, I like this song," I'd announce.

"I hate this song," someone would retort.

So, I'd be all, "Okay, I don't like it either."

That's why Goosehead is so important to me. It's expanded my world enough to make me realize it doesn't matter what anybody thinks! If you think something's cool, it's cool. There are so many different types of people on Goosehead that not everyone likes the same things. Or feels the need to fit in. Makes for interesting fun on the boards.

And another thing—it's just a song. Or it's just an outfit. It's minor. Who cares what anyone thinks about it?

These words are easier to say than to live by. But what I've learned is, while you can't help what people think or say about you, you can take responsibility for your response. And you can create your own social circle, choosing friends who love you as is instead of yearning to be part of an intolerant clique.

Finally, you can cultivate your own independence—learn to love your friends but not rely on them. I did that by creating Goosehead on my own. You can do it by, say, vowing to spend some daily time by yourself—reading, drawing, taking a walk, whatever. Or by taking on some responsibility, whether it's an after school job or a spot on a sports team.

It may seem like a contradiction, but I think independence is the most attractive quality a friend can have.

Enter Kristin, Brittany,
Megan, and Tootsa . . .

Enter Kristin, Brittany, Megan, and Tootsa . . .

You know how I said nothing can replace history? Well, there are those few people you meet and immediately feel like you've known them your entire life. Enter Megan, Kristin, Brittany, and Tootsa. My entire high school experience has been filled with more laughter and smiles with these special four in my life. We are each so different that we bring out the best in each other. We met freshman year. I had math with Megan, PE with Kris, computer class with Britt, and religion with Tootsa. I took Kristin to a premiere party, and as we danced and raged into the wee hours we instantly became friends. Whenever I was absent from math class, I always remember Megan writing my missed assignments on cute notes and always saying hello. Tootsa's great sense of humor was hard to miss in class, and even though we sat across the

"WHATEVER"

Recipe for Girls' Night In

Female bonding with my buds is never complete without our drug of choice—junk food.

It's the essential ingredient to all sleep-overs, after-school hang time, and phone chats.

A menu . . .

- Homemade cookies (Brittany eats the middles only, which annoys Megan no end)
- Crush soda
- Cactus Cooler
- Peach rings
- Gummi Worms
- Fruit snacks
- Chocolate
- Goldfish crackers
- Ice cream with crushed Girl Scout cookies (Kristin is the chef for this dish)
- Grapes
- And my famous eggs—I will never tell you my secret ingredient

43

room, we were always talking somehow. By Christmas vacation we were buds. What made us best friends? Our first "Girls' Night In." The first few were very much steeped in ritual. We had a list of things we did every time. As time went by we had "Girls' Nights Out." We all got cars, had boys in and out of our lives, and so now with all of our hectic schedules a Girls' Night is just all of us together doing whatever we can for the night. Still, I am convinced that first Girls' Night sealed our friendship.

"WHATEVER"

We figured, if boys can have a Guys' Night Out, we can have a Girls' Night In.

We used to start by singing goofy songs as we got into our pajamas. Next we'd set up our grub. We chilled Strawberry Crush soda (the bottled kind is a must), and Megan and I would always bake something, like chocolate-chip cookies. While the cookies were baking we would arduously select a movie from the Blockbuster-sized DVD collection we have at my house.

Then we'd chow down on our huge stock of junk food, watch flicks, and talk and talk and talk.

All of us girls sleep in my little queen bed. (We're all tall and we all kick!) Usually one or two of us bail and end up snoozing on a couch.

We sleep in, then grab our sunglasses and purses and walk in our pajamas to Bob's Big Boy, three blocks away, for breakfast.

Anything goes at our Girls' Nights In except drugs and drama because we have more fun without them. Sure, sometimes the talk gets heavy and there are tears all around, but mostly we're bonding over laughter and getting rejuvenated before another long week at school.

Growing Apart

Growing Apart

Like a favorite pair of old shoes that start pinching at the toes, sometimes you grow out of certain friendships. You might hobble around in those too tight shoes for a while, but eventually you have to face the inevitable and put them in the giveaway pile.

We all change as we age and grow, and sometimes the people around grow differently—at a different rate or in a different direction. As I have experienced this, I've realized it's not in my hands. Instead of worrying and upsetting myself, I need to let things be what they are. I try to judge people and situations less as I grow, and the first step is doing this with the people around me. It can be hard, but when it happens to me, I try to remember all the good that person brought to my life and the fun we had. Even if they're not around, my memories are priceless.

You Talking to Me?

You Talking to Me?

I've had some epic battles with friends. And more than once I've heard through the high school grapevine: "So-and-so is gonna kick Ashley Power's ass." (Okay, I haven't been in a fistfight since I graduated from the nursery-school sandbox, so this threat is clearly empty. And I hope it remains that way.)

HONK!!!

There ought to be a place on the teen food pyramid for drama, because we thrive on it. We've gotta have it. If there isn't some drama in our lives—a big breakup, some parental injustice, a huge humiliation—we'll create it.

I think that's the source of a lot of squabbles between me and my friends. Our stress and frustration just explodes, and whoever is in the way had better watch out.

But mostly, fights are fought by proxy. It's the typical "He said that she said that you said" crap. This has taught me, number one, to keep my mouth shut. It seems no matter what I say gets twisted around so that I look like a witch. I could say, Rachel's skirt looks cute on her. And later she'll come up and say, "Kelly said you told her I look like an ugly whore!" I'd rather keep my thoughts to myself than get in some screaming match based on a communication problem. Usually in these situations I just stop the fighting before the voices are raised.

I'd say, "Rachel, stay here, I'll be right back." Then I'd grab Kelly, pull her over to Rachel, and confront the two of them until they realized the problem was between them because someone was obviously lying.

This could have evolved into an all-day drama, feeding the gossip mill and entertaining the entire tenth grade. But alas, I stopped the play before it had a fighting chance.

A little bit of drama is good, but is a long, drawn-out fight really how you want to spend an entire school day? If not, I recommend my slightly embarrassing, but highly effective, confrontational model of stopping fights in their tracks.

Friends or Guys?
Friends or Girls?

When your hormones go into overdrive over a new crush, it's tempting to devote every minute to him or her. In other words, blow off your friends in favor of swapping spit.

This is a big mistake. I learned it the hard way when I met a guy who I fell for . . . hard. Soon my schedule was planned around when I could see him, and trust me, that lasted all of two seconds. When my friends caught on, they were the first to give me a little wakeup call. They were upset because I was breaking plans with them for his beck 'n' call. It's funny, a couple of weeks later he had moved on to his new flavor of the month, and I wasn't all that important anymore. But my friends never left me. That's what I remember when I'm dating a new guy. When he leaves, my friends will still be there.

No matter how smitten you are, balancing friendship with romance is essential. And not just because significant others tend to evaporate overnight. The main reason is quality of life. Time with friends, family, a

"WHATEVER"
The Perils of Fame . . .

Kristin, Brittany, Megan, and Tootsa are total Goosehead cheerleaders. They keep up with changes on the site and sympathize when I'm overloaded with work. They've even been known to show up in episodes of *Whatever* or at photo shoots.

I know how this might look. I cringe every time I hear about a star who hires his friends to be "managers" or pays them simply to join his entourage. The word is *sycophant*.

But that's so not the arrangement with my friends and me. For one, they all have lives of their own. The last thing they need to do is latch onto someone else's career. What's more, when all the Goosehead attention dies down, as it inevitably does from time to time, my buds are still there for me.

That's not always the case with other friends.

Sometimes, right after my picture shows up in some magazine, I'll get phone calls from people I haven't seen in ages. Suddenly they want to hang out again. That sucks! You think, *Cool, I remember you,* then it turns to, *Can you do this for me? Let's get together.*

Usually I politely rely on my "I'm too busy" line and get off the phone quick. With friends like that, who needs the paparazzi?

boyfriend, yourself—they're all essential. Let one of these things edge out the others, and your life will start to resemble a dull, monochromatic blob.

I couldn't live in such a one-note world. That's why I've never allowed myself to lose that balance again. Yep, wonder boy was the first, and last, guy to sweep me off my firmly planted feet. My friends are a gift more important than any Saturday-night date or moment in the spotlight could be. I won't let anything—not a guy or a hectic work schedule or Goosehead fame—come between me and my buds.

If you judge people, you have no time to love them.
—Mother Teresa

GolDeN Egg

Getting ready for my ninth-grade dance

Chapter Four
Let's Talk About Love—
AAAAAAAHHHHHH

When exactly did boys stop being gross and started looking, well, hot? Though it feels like I've been ogling guys, obsessing about guys, and dating guys forever, I wasn't always a boy-crazy babe.

Until I was about twelve, in fact, I was an average boy-loathing, tomboyish kid.

Take my annual visits to my dad and his family in Missouri. With each visit, we'd always pick up where we left off, talking about school, sports, music, Mom, and other scintillating stuff. I was way more interested in basketball than boys. My world was about surviving seventh-grade math and working out with my b-ball teammates. My social life consisted of sleep-overs with girlfriends. Boys? They were simply annoying people who lived to harass you on the playground and gross you out at lunch.

This was the me that my dad had always known.

But the summer of 1998, when I was thirteen, things changed. It was something I was barely conscious of—until I saw my dad's head start to spin.

The week was cruising along as it usually does—plenty of hang time and ice-cream runs with my stepsister, Whitney, and a lot of family dinners. Then one afternoon, the doorbell rang. And standing on the front porch were a few guys I knew from the neighborhood, shuffling their big feet and asking for me. Except this summer, they weren't interested in teasing me or playing a game of Horse at our driveway basketball hoop. They were just . . . interested.

And I was psyched! I bounded outside in full flirt mode and had a great time chatting with the guys.

Well, Dad sort of freaked.

When we finally talked about it, he admitted that the guy time had worried him. And this wasn't just his Mormon conservatism talking.

"I don't want you to think you're a circus show," he said. "All that attention could overwhelm you."

What are you talking about? Hello! That's exactly what I wanted. Little did Dad know—I craved that attention like it was chocolate-chip-cookie-dough ice cream.

"Do you even understand what it is to be a thirteen-year-old girl?" I remember asking him. "We live for guys."

At sixteen, I can definitely say that I no longer need a guy's admiration to feel worthy. I'll blame my mood swings on Goosehead's ups and downs, school stress, or hormones long before I'll give a dude credit for them.

Still, when it comes to my fave extracurriculars, dating does top my list. Perhaps it's because guys are the ultimate challenge. They're like the last frontier you hear about in old Westerns. They're an utter mystery that I've barely begun to decode.

Not that I won't try in this chapter. . . .

Crushing

Crushing

Okay, I admit it—I used to live in the throes of DiCaprio dementia. I mean, who didn't? None of my friends could resist Leo's strung-out poet of *The Basketball Diaries*. And when Leo did Shakespeare with Claire Danes? Romeo, Romeo, wherefore art thou Romeo, indeed.

So, is this a bad thing? If I had plastered my room with Leo's face, spent hours in Leo fan sites, or thought of Leo as someone I knew, instead of an actor I admired, then yeah, maybe it would have been.

But I think I had my Leo crush under control. He was just something to gush about during girlfriend phone time. He made going to the movies that much more fun. He was a good-looking fantasy boy, like a Ken doll who studied method acting and dated supermodels.

It was no big thing.

Crushes on guys who actually live in my world could be different. It's not inconceivable that that high school quarterback with the mysterious eyes and the big muscles could ask me out. Right?

But to tell you the truth, I might be disappointed if he actually did.

A crush exists to star in your daydreams. He or she is someone to look up to, someone who seems perfect. They're ideals, as far away from the nuts and bolts of real life as possible. I think that's why so many fans go gaga over movie stars and rock idols.

Okay, so what happens if I start dating my crush? I find out he's

Mystery is exciting, mystery is dangerous, mystery is so powerful, yet subtle in form.
—A close and wise friend

GolDeN Egg

always crabby before homeroom, he hates my favorite *Seinfeld* episode, and he has a bad habit of chugging Surge and burping really really loudly. He becomes . . . a boyfriend, totally reality based. Boyfriends are great and all, but if your starry-eyed crush becomes one, you might find yourself wishing you had that fantasy boy back.

I think that's why I've been known to crush on unattainable people. When I was in fourth grade, I spotted James on the first day of school. I was smitten. He was four feet eleven and had blond hair and blue eyes, and he wore the cutest little suit. He was my dream boy! But we were in fourth grade; nothing would happen.

So when I found out James liked me back, I got really confused. James was my crush—he wasn't supposed to like me back. This ruined everything!

Well, actually, what it did was cure me of my crush. He got over the fact that I didn't like him that way, and James and I eventually became friends. Still, if he liked anyone else, I was always so jealous. It was so confusing, and at eight years old I figured this whole love thing would be better when I was sixteen. It isn't. And I have a feeling the glitches won't be cured for a while. The system is so messed up. You like a guy you've only seen at school and have never spoken to him. Every time he walks by, you swoon and wish he'd look at you. You find out he has a girlfriend. A junior named Molly. The competition begins. You set yourself up for failure. But then, if by chance he begins liking you, he calls you every day, walks you to your classes, buys you lunch, agrees with everything you say, and insists he loves you when he's known you one week. I don't know about you, but I'd be over it in a day. It's my personality. I like the chase.

Getting perspective on the whole crush phenom is easier when you've been the object of a crush. And as a result of Goosehead, I have been known to get a swoony e-mail or two. I always read these e-mails with a wary eye.

I know the dude's got it together if he, say, responds to a Goosehead feature or something I said in my advice column. Or maybe he'll compliment me on some Goosehead press that he's seen.

It's when the e-mails take up more than one screen or the guy starts getting a little too presumptuous—suggesting that we are soul mates, perhaps—that I know he's lost control of his crush. That's a bit disturbing.

It's also a great way to remind myself that a crush is a crush is a crush—it's best left in fantasyland with your unicorns and that five pounds you keep saying you're going to lose.

"WHATEVER"

Classic Signs of a Crush
I always know I've entered crush territory
when I do these slightly ridiculous things . . .

- Get all glammed up to see the object of my affection play football, even though, Hello! He's going to be playing football. He's not going to even see me.
- Speculate with my girlfriends about my crush's favorite color, his favorite food, his favorite shoes . . . you get the idea.
- Blush and feel my heart rate double when I see him in the hall.
- If I actually speak to him, I don't hear a word he says because I'm too busy wondering if there's lipstick on my teeth.
- Doodle my crush's name in the margins of my homework.
- Forget his name the minute a new crush crosses my path.

Attraction

Attraction

Most girls can describe their perfect guys as if they were items on a diner menu: "Yes, I'd like a cheeseburger, medium well, no onions, please. And on the side, I'll take a guy about six feet tall with dark brown hair, really white teeth, and a not annoying laugh. No mullets."

Guys are no different. Ask any guy whether he prefers a Cameron Diaz type to a Jennifer Love Hewitt, and he'll be able to give you a very detailed description of his dream babe.

So, I'll admit it. I have an ideal, too. He'd be a tall, sexy Brad Pitt type with crystal-blue eyes, sandy-blond hair, and a great smile.

Have I gone out with guys who actually look like this? Not really. Because the minute I get to know someone, my "type" flies out the window. Looks don't matter nearly as much as the stuff beneath the surface.

For me, first and foremost, a guy's got to be intelligent—someone who can hold his own in a conversation that's not about wrestling or the latest mall gossip.

Independence is another priority. No matter how much I dig a guy with good orthodontia and an awesome car, I wouldn't want a guy to agree with everything I say just because. If he has his own opinions, goals, and dreams, he's going to be attractive, regardless of whether or not he hates Dr Pepper.

And he's going to want the same thing in his significant other.

Those are the qualities I strive for. Do I want to please a guy I'm interested in? Sure. By making time in my schedule for him, laughing at his jokes, quizzing him before the SATs. But asking me to change my thoughts is out of line.

In other words, for guys or girls, I think the ideal match is someone who will take you as is.

Games People Play . . .

Games People Play

When it comes to love, everybody says they don't play games. But you know what? Everybody does.

And guess what else? I don't have a problem with this. To me, dating is about the journey (having fun with a guy on a Friday night) and not the destination (snagging a boyfriend). If you look at it that way, the mind games we play with boys (and they with us) are half the fun.

Which is why I've devised a list of dating rules. They're not from some man-manipulating book and they're not for everybody. They're simply the techniques that work for me. Although my love life's been pretty pathetic of late. So take everything I say with a grain of salt.

1. I don't kiss on the first date. After one date, how can you know if you really like this person? Besides, leaving your date smoochless may also leave him or her intrigued.

2. Keep your date talking. Let them talk about themselves. Everyone likes to listen to themselves talk. Just add enough to keep the conversation going. Yes, this may stroke his or her ego, but it's also the best way for you to learn a thing or two about him or her. That way, you can figure out if you want to pursue date number two.

3. Don't clear your weekend schedule because you're hoping Mr. or Ms. Right's going to ask you out. Make your suitors work with your (busy) social calendar.

4. Don't be afraid to ask him/her out! All they can say is no. Which they do, a lot of the time.

5. Don't kiss and tell. In fact, don't tell, period. Not only will this endear you to any gossip-averse dates, but it will also protect you from the influence of well-meaning friends.

Scenario: You get home from a date and immediately dial your buds on three-way. You spend the next hour thoroughly dissecting the date. Everybody weighs in with an opinion or three. And by the time you hang up the phone, you're so confused, you don't know what you think of your prospective significant other.

That's why I try to keep my thoughts to myself when I'm mulling over a new dude. Honestly, I usually talk to Mark. He is the God of Advice. He's been in the same spot as these studs I'm dating, so he's good at telling me what's up and what I should do next. Sometimes my girlfriends call and ask Mark what they should do with their dudes.

How to Ask a Guy Out . . . .

People look at me and say, "How many boyfriends have you had? Thousands?" Actually, no. I never get asked out.

My mother said recently that if nobody asks me to homecoming, she was going to pay someone to do it. Thanks for the vote of confidence, Mom!

I have to think it's because guys are intimidated by my Web celeb. Or maybe I'm an alien from another planet. Either way, if I want a date on Saturday night, sometimes I have to take matters into my own hands.

**Desire, ask, believe, receive.
—Stella Terril Mann**

GolDeN Egg

1. I think asking someone out in person is sometimes easier than the phone. You can have a nice, intimate conversation and read their body language. So, I walk up to the guy at school—but only if he's by himself. Approaching a guy or girl in a group puts too much pressure on both of you! It also feeds the ever-hungry high-school gossip monster.

2. Then I'll simply say, "My name's Ashley. I'm a sophomore. You don't know me and I don't know you, but I'd like to get to know you. Can we go out and have coffee or have lunch?"

3. If he hems and haws, I jump in quickly and say, "Okay, no problem. If you don't want to go out, I understand. I just thought I'd ask." This makes you look confident and makes it easier to brush off this small rejection.

4. If your date accepts, nail down a day and time right then, like coffee after school or lunch over the weekend. (These are ideal, casual first-date options.) If you don't commit to a time, the opportunity could be lost in a sea of phone tag and unanswered e-mails.

5. In my book, the person who does the asking ought to pay. But if a girl asks a guy out, yet he jumps to pay when she reaches for her wallet, he's scoring major points. He's also probably indicating that he's had fun and would like to go out again. Seize the day and suggest date number two.

Everybody Wants a Boyfriend or Girlfriend . . .

Right? Well, actually, I prefer flying solo.

What? You might ask. Forgive me, Ash, but you seem as boy crazy as the next girl.

That's true. And that's exactly why I don't want a boyfriend. I'd much rather play the field.

I mean, imagine a life in which you'd only tasted one fruit—an apple. Your first taste of a mango or kiwi might make you forget that apples ever existed. But you'll never know that unless you take that first taste of something new.

That's how I feel about committing to one person at such a young age.

How can you know you want to spend the rest of your life (or even the rest of your high-school years) with someone if you've only dated one or two people, ever?

I think a lot of people seek the comfort of a relationship in high school because they're afraid of getting hurt. Who isn't? But I think that pain is an important

TaKe a GanDer @

The Universe Is a Green Dragon:
A Cosmic Creation Story,
by Brian Swimme

My favorite part of this book is a conversation between a boy and his mentor, who tells him something like, "You want in life to become love. And to become love, you have to fall in love as deeply and as often as possible. You have to get hurt. That's part of growing and learning and trying."

thing to go through. Why else would falling in love be called, well, falling in love? You fall for someone, and as in any plunge, you might wipe out in the dirt. If that happens, you get up, you learn a little, and you try again.

You don't get to learn much if you only fall once.

Playing the field also protects you from getting trapped in a mock marriage. I've seen too many serious relationships between teens get out of control. They go from committed to controlling, from passionate to petulant.

Some guys are insecure and easily jealous of my guy friends. To which I'd simply reply, "Get over it. I'm with you, not them, right? So there's nothing to worry about."

If having a boyfriend or girlfriend is fun and enriching—great. But if it's a lot of angst and accusations, I think I'll wait for adulthood, thank you very much.

Someday I'll be ready to commit to another person and adapt my life to fit his. But right now, I live for myself and my family. My independence is more important to me than a steady, Saturday-night date.

HONK!!!

I usually date older guys. Possibly because I am always around people older than I am. Though it makes my mom nuts, the guys I'm attracted to tend not to be my exact age. After running a company and dealing with daily sixteen-year-old drama, I think I earn the right to be treated with respect. When a dude I'm dating calls me immature or talks to me like I'm a baby . . . oh, he might as well drop me off at home and forget my number. That's one thing I can't deal with. I've worked very hard. If you want to get to date number two, don't act like you're doing the girl or guy a favor. And don't make yourself feel more adequate by making others feel bad about themselves.

"WHATEVER"

My Two-Guy Debacle

I learned an important lesson recently—before you date two guys at once, find out if they're friends. I think this one is self-explanatory. Basically, I got busted big time! I thought I was being slick.

One guy was out of town, so I was chillin' with dude number two. Of course when number one got home, he called number two. It wasn't pretty. I think my exact words were: "#*&%." It's just not worth it.

My Number-One Weapon

My eighth-grade English teacher, Mrs. Sauvé, scared me to death at first. But she was also a very wise woman. She was always dropping little life lessons in her students' laps, smack-dab in the middle of some Odyssey lecture. She did it so subtly that half the class probably missed her helpful hints.

But I was navigating junior high at a new school, and I needed all the help I could get. So every time Mrs. Sauvé dropped one of her golden eggs, I listened hard. This is one I've never forgotten:

"The things only you know are like a wall around you," she said one day, "If you share those things, the walls begin to crumble, leaving you vulnerable to the world."

I've lived my life by those words. There are things in my head that I haven't even told my best girlfriends. Maybe someday I will, but I don't feel a burning desire to unload all my secrets. I like keeping some things to myself.

In the cutthroat world of high school politics, this is definitely smart policy. You never know when a former friend and confidante is going to whip out some embarrassing bit of information and stab you in the back with it.

Discretion is even more important in the dating world. The things you choose to keep to yourself—who you're crushing on, who you hooked up with at that party last week, how serious you were with your last boyfriend—do more than protect you from the gossip mill. They also envelop you with mystery.

And mystery is incredibly attractive. Why else would women always fall for a brooding, bad-boy type or the strong silent guy? Just as everyone wants to unravel a riddle, we're all intrigued by a mysterious mate.

In my experience, the best way to make someone want to know you is to be just a little bit unknowable.

GolDeN Egg

Mom and I are as close as we can get.

Chapter Five
Body, Body
Physique Mystique

It's hard to believe my mom and I have the same genes. She's fair and freckly, and I'm tan. Mom's body is petite, compact, and skinny, while I'm tall and voluptuous.

Have I ever wished that I had inherited my mom's perky little genes over my dad's big bearish ones? I'd be lying if I said no. Today it seems many things are based on appearance. A girl has to be a size 2 to model for Guess? A guy has to have a six-pack to be an Abercrombie & Fitch star. All around us we see people who must match certain criteria to be "pretty" or "handsome."

So much value is placed on the outside that I think in the shuffle of eating disorders and depression, it's possible to lose ourselves. My body is what they call "flawed." I have curves, extra weight, hips, breasts, broad shoulders, long legs, big feet. I'm no size 2; I'm not a size 4. And you know what, I never will be. It's not in my bone structure. Even if I went on a crash diet and became an exercise fiend, I wouldn't be a size 4. And that's okay.

I try to eat healthy, and I started exercising more. It's hard to get outta bed at seven A.M. during vacation and head to the gym on an empty stomach for a two-hour workout. But I feel better afterward and it's a nice feeling of accomplishment.

But I'm not going to tell you how easy it is to love yourself as you are. Because I don't think it's that easy. I still struggle with accepting myself. We all find faults within ourselves; some are really there. Some we make up. Some are visible. Some only we can see. Here are some of my flaws. Some I have conquered. Some I'm still working on.

* I'm a mumbler.
* I'm a procrastinator.
* I'm very hard on myself.
* Sometimes I don't give myself enough credit.
* I'm a fixer.
* I'm not skinny enough.
* I'm not assertive enough.
* I have immense fear of failure.
* I don't always love myself.
* I want to be loved.
* I'm scared of letting down my parents.

That's not it; there's more, I'm sure. You see, we are all our biggest critic. I am more critical of myself and body than anyone I know. I have to get over that. I have to work to get where I feel good about myself. Not because I want my ex to realize how beautiful I am or because I want to "fit in" at school. For me. It has to be for me and no one else.

It's been especially hard to accept myself since Goosehead has taken off. I get lots of people on my site and lots of e-mails. More good e-mails than bad, but the bad ones can really sting. Critical letters. Criticizing my credibility. My looks. Calling me fat. Saying I'm ugly. I should look in a mirror. I should stop eating.

I am a human being. And it's not so easy to brush off an e-mail like that. It hurts my feelings. Makes me doubt myself and my capabilities. But I don't feel sorry for myself. I don't wallow in self-pity. I take a deep breath and move on. It's someone's opinion. Someone I don't even know.

Never did I claim to be Kate Moss. I just want to be me. I want to show every girl out there that it is okay to not look like a Victoria's Secret model.

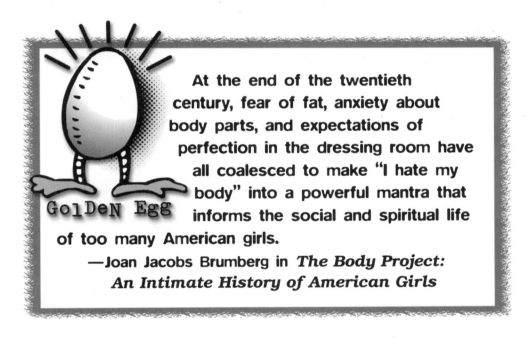

GolDeN Egg

At the end of the twentieth century, fear of fat, anxiety about body parts, and expectations of perfection in the dressing room have all coalesced to make "I hate my body" into a powerful mantra that informs the social and spiritual life of too many American girls.
—Joan Jacobs Brumberg in *The Body Project: An Intimate History of American Girls*

"WHATEVER"

Walk Like a (Wo)Man . . .

L.A. shelters more Barbie Doll bodies per square mile than any other city on earth, I think. I've seen plenty of girls who walk down the street, looking like supermodels on their way home from a *Cosmo* shoot. (Who knows, maybe they are.)

But that doesn't mean they walk with confidence. Some of them walk hunched over, with terminal shy-girl posture. Or they take little, mincing steps—maybe that's all they can manage in their teetering, spike-heeled shoes. Or they cover their mouths with their hands or futz with their hair or pull at their shirts.

I've got to tell you—all that self-conscious fidgeting really chips away at these girls' beauty. (Guy friends have confirmed this, by the way.)

This has made me realize that it doesn't really matter what size I am, or how perfect my legs are, or how blond my hair is. Being pretty is about being confident, about literally being comfortable in your own skin. It's about not caring about a bad-hair day (or at least acting like you don't). It's about not comparing yourself to anyone.

Now, I've never in my life walked around the house with books on my head or given a thought to the way I carry myself. But people have told me that I walk, stand, and even flop onto the couch (which I do a lot) with a lot of confidence.

That makes sense because I am comfortable in my own skin.

This is not to say I look in the mirror every morning and say, *"Magnifique."* But I do think enough of myself that I can shrug off my imperfections, slap some cover-up on that zit, and walk out the door.

Do I care what people think of my appearance? Sure. But I care more about my own comfort level.

And maybe that's where my beauty lies.

A washboard stomach and cut arms do not make someone handsome. You could have the most beautiful body, but if there's nothing inside, it doesn't matter. My body may not be perfect, but it's mine. Yes, I'll never be Kate Moss, but she'll never be me.

Zits on My Image . . .

Like every other teenager, I get the occasional zit. I hate them, but I get them, especially once a month when I'm PMS-ing.

This should be just one of those mildly annoying symptoms of adolescence. But since I'm the "face of Goosehead.com," breaking out can be a serious liability.

If I'm in a meeting with a studio head, for instance, and he sees a zit on my face, I can just feel him freaking out inside.

It's unfair! If an adult went into a meeting with a zit on his/her head, no one would even care!

What's worse is, once you're in the public eye, people are always on the lookout for such flaws. Drew Barrymore's too chubby, Calista Flockhart's too skinny, J-Lo's wearing no clothes . . . the criticism goes on and on.

I met Britney Spears last year at a party after her LA concert. She was fabulous—beautiful, cool, and confident and interesting. But when I reported back to my friends, one blurted out, "Oh my gosh, I heard she has bad skin! Does she?!?"

"Hey," I retorted, "look at your skin. Do you break out? Well, Britney Spears is nineteen—I'm sure she breaks out, too."

And you know what? She's allowed to be human. So am I. And if that means I get a zit every once in a while or I decide to go to the drugstore in ripped-up sweats or I look goofy on the Goosehead Web cam, so be it.

The irony is, I also get slammed by Goosehead users for being too perfect. Publicity photos that are touched up so my skin looks velvety, my hair completely unmussed, and my teeth whiter than white are part of the oppressive media culture, say the critics.

Stephanie Joy Pruner put it best in a ranting e-mail to Goosehead: "I'm tired of seeing a million pictures of Ashley looking like a !#%&$! super-model."

When I got that harsh letter, I checked out Stephanie's own home page, found it to be as brilliant as green acid, and asked her to become a Goosehead teen columnist.

Man, was she surprised.

In her first column, next to a picture of me with a mustache and a blackened tooth, she wrote:

I now realize that the photos are for appeal of the site and to attract visitors (ahem, this means you, fellas!), but that probably doesn't make you girls feel any better. The thing is, we should say, "I'm happy with the way I was born." I know it sounds totally cliché, but it's true! Someone tell me, has wishing you were someone else gotten you ANYWHERE, ever?

I'm just as conflicted about my public image as Stephanie is. I'm cursed if I look pretty and cursed if I don't. I'm blamed if there are too many photos of me on Goosehead.com and blamed if there are too few.

Of course, my experience is just an extreme version of walking the halls at school every day, where the scrutiny and criticism of people's appearance can be vicious.

GolDeN Egg

Stephanie's right. Stressing about your zits, or whatever other figure flaws are angsting you out that day, is futile. It's not going to make that zit go away. So, what do you do? It sounds goofy, but . . . take ownership of your zits! Don't be ashamed! Just laugh it off. Chances are, others will, too.

Working Out

Last year, I started working out with a trainer, Eric, a big, lanky former football player with a completely Californian personality. Over the summer, when my schedule was school-free, Eric and I would meet for two hours every morning at the gym near my house.

I loved Eric's workouts. I mean, sometimes I hated them because they were so grueling. But I can say I always loved having finished one.

Eric was fond of having me do sit-ups while tossing a medicine ball over my head to the point of exhaustion. Another favorite was balancing on a giant ball using nothing but my abs to support myself. We also did arduous water aerobics, using weights and floats.

But these workouts weren't just a bod-toning project. They were a refuge from my day—from work, parents, traffic, baby brother, whatever. When I exercise, stress seems to flow out of my body along with the sweat. I get a real sense of peace.

Eric says it's the endorphins released during exercise that make you so mellow after a workout. I think it's also the sense of simple accomplishment: you lifted a weight twenty times. How basic, how beautiful is that?

True, sometimes I love the solitude of a long swim in the lap pool, where I can just work my muscles and think. But mostly, exercising with my trainer or a friend is the best way to motivate, to have fun, and get the job done. It's become an important part of my lifestyle and the swiftest avenue to both physical and mental health.

Food

Nobody is supposed to be more conflicted about food than teenage girls. And believe me, I've seen my share of eating disorders among my friends.

But I mostly eat what I want, whether it's a turkey sandwich with cheese (my fave lunch), a sweet after-school snack, or a groaning Mexican dinner. Is this because eating never makes me gain weight? Not even. Like any woman, I worry about how I look, and I make the connection between that extra pudding cup and that extra five pounds.

But to tell you the truth, I don't usually sweat it enough to give up the pudding cup if I really want it.

People who won't let a speck of chocolate ice cream cross their lips because they fear the fat grams will kill them freak me out.

Take a Gander @

Bitchen in the Kitchen: The PMS Survival Cookbook, by Jennifer Evans and Fritzi Horstman Like anyone with a mom who cooks, I need major motivation to whip out a chef's knife. But as many of you well know, there's no motivation like the agonies of PMS—the bloating, the crankiness, and those mega–chocolate cravings (as opposed to those mega Fritos cravings). So when I'm waiting for my "little friend" and truly bummin', I whip out these goofy recipes for soothing edibles, feel-good facials, and the like.

At the end of the day I don't ask myself, How many fat grams did I consume? Let's count the calories. Instead I wonder, Do I have enough energy? Do I feel good? Do I look in the mirror and like what I see?

If not, I might step up my exercise or watch what I eat for a while. But I don't let it take over my life. I enjoy eating too much for that!

Take a Gander @

Succulent Wild Woman: Dancing with Your Wonder Full Self, by Sark
This book is handwritten and beautifully painted by this wacky, wonderful artist, Sark. It's a book full of affirmations, telling women to love their cellulite, embrace life, conquer their fears, and stuff like that. But unlike some "women's books," this one doesn't take itself too seriously—it's funny and self-deprecating and uplifting in a very real way. A total pick-me-up. She also wrote *The Bodacious Book of Succulence: Daring to Live Your Succulent Wild Life.*

Drugs

Before I even started ninth grade, I decided I was going to get through high school without ever trying drugs. I was inspired by a friend, a high school senior, who'd made the same pledge.

"People gave me a hard time," he told me. "I heard a lot of crap about it. But you know, it's cool to be a senior and be able to say, I've never done that."

On one level, this is an easy vow for me to make because I hate to lose control of myself. I've seen enough friends flopping around at parties, their heads lolling, their eyes rolling, and their reputations disintegrating like sand castles in a typhoon, to know that drugs are not for me.

Getting high is also not worth all the risks. If you're not in control of yourself, you're not going to check to see if the person driving you home is sober. Or you may not be able to fend off an unwanted groper. You could, in other words, find yourself in serious physical and emotional danger.

Just as I approach sex by thinking about the consequences, I can't help but think about the repercussions of doing drugs. So many things could happen—addiction, falling into financial ruin, hurting people you love, getting into serious legal trouble.

What's fun about that kind of high?

The Hard Facts About Hard Liquor

Okay, all those things I just said about drugs? They also apply to drink. But let's face it, in the teen culture, drinking is far more prevalent and accepted than drug use. I'm not saying this is a good thing—it's just a fact. Almost all teenagers drink. And we don't do that one-beer-at-happy-hour thing like some adults. We drink to get drunk. It's like, five beers or none.

It's smartest not to drink at all. But given the reality of alcohol in our lives, if you choose to do it, be smart:

• Always have a designated driver who doesn't touch one drop of alcohol.

• If your parents will pitch a fit if you call them at 2 A.M. saying, "I'm drunk and I need a ride home," or even if you say, "My driver is drunk and I need a ride home," then make sure you go out with someone whose parents don't have a zero-tolerance policy.
Like . . . my parents. My mom and Mark, of course, do not want me to drink. But more than anything, their priority is that I stay safe, that I never get in a car with someone who's been drinking. That's why we have a rule—if I ever need a safe ride, I can call them for one, no matter how late the hour.

• Emergency bail code. My friends and I decide on a specific emergency word of the night. Say, *licorice* is our emergency word. If someone in our group is trapped with a scary guy or in an uncomfortable spot, all they gotta do is yell, "Hey, can you grab the licorice!" and we'll get them out of there fast. Make up an urgent page. Or a "Can you help me find the bathroom?" Anything to rescue a friend.

Lighting Up . . .

Lighting Up . . .

My parents would kill me if I ever started smoking cigarettes. Why? Because they smoke themselves. "Do as I say, not as I do" (Mark's favorite saying). It's an object lesson. I look at my parents and see how hard it is to quit smoking once you're addicted to nicotine. And it helps me resist the urge to ever start.

My rebellion against conformity also keeps me nic-free. At my high school, smoking is currently the thing to do. My classmates love saying, "Oh, I need a smoke." They love that holding-the-butt-with-two-fingers thing. They adore the luxurious inhaling and exhaling. This kind of cool is so lame! I can't bring myself to buy into it.

The thing I don't understand about smoking is why people start in the first place. It's no lie how detrimental smoking is to your body, and no one wants to kiss an ashtray!

My guess is people start smoking to look cool, to fit in, or to have something to do with their nervous hands. And then they continue to smoke because they get hooked on the nicotine. It's a pretty vicious cycle without much reward.

To me, a smoking habit is the opposite of

standing on your own two feet, like using any drug. And that's the best argument I can think of for swearing off all drugs.

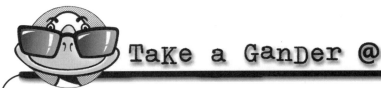

Take a Gander @

Here are some sites to get more information about substance abuse:

National Council on Alcoholism and Drug Dependence:
www.ncadd.org/facts/youdir.html

For families and friends of Alcoholics:
www.al-anon.alateen.org

Narcotics Anonymous: www.na.org

National Drug Abuse Hotline: 1-800-662-4357
Hopeline hotline referral: 1-800-NCA-CALL

Sex

Okay, we've established that adolescence can wreak havoc on your body. You shoot up taller in bizarre spurts. Your skin goes spotty. Your hips flare so fast, you get stretch marks. And then there's the dreaded "awkward phase," where your nose seems to outgrow the rest of your face, your feet swell to size 9 while the rest of your bod is still a size 2, or you gain fifteen pounds in one semester.

But all that surface stuff is nothing compared to the earthquake rumbling inside your bod.

I'm talking, of course, about hormones. Raging ones.

These stealthy little scoundrels not only make you crabby when you're PMS-ing or make your voice crack right in the middle of that student-council campaign speech. They can also make you want to grab the closest person of the opposite (or not) sex and lick him or her all over. Like, during Spanish class.

Not only do hormones mess with our loins, they fool with our heads. They help a crush become true love in a record six minutes. They make us forget about curfew the instant we touch first base. They urge us to say, "Yes, yes, a thousand times yes," when maybe, we shouldn't be saying any such thing.

So, about the whole sex question for me? I'll admit it—I've experienced seven in heaven and wondered what I could do with ten. I've been tempted.

So, let's be real. The chances that I'm going to wait until I'm married to do it are slim. But that doesn't mean I take sex lightly.

One reason for that is my mom, who was eighteen when she had me. Though I know she wouldn't change the circumstances of my birth, I also know my mother didn't exactly plan to be married with a baby before her nineteenth birthday.

Some teenagers seem to have a magical switch in their brains. They turn it on and somehow forget that sex can lead to pregnancy. Thankfully, I don't have that switch!

Okay, and what about STDs? We're the most sexually educated generation in history. I got my first dose of sex ed well before I was ten years old. I know all about HIV and herpes and how they're transmitted. I know what a dental dam is, even though I've never seen one!

"WHATEVER"
Why I'm Waiting . . .

A lot of us live in this vague state called Not Ready. But what does that mean, really? To me, it means that I don't yet have the maturity to get seriously involved with someone without losing part of myself—my individuality and my focus on work and family. Until I feel I can balance my passions with my sense of self, I'm going to wait.

Anybody who can disregard all that scary information to take a light-hearted roll in the hay is not thinking. And if there's anything I always do, it's think before I pounce.

So here's what I think: To me, sex is giving of yourself in a big way. And in keeping with my High-School Relationships Should Be Fun and Lighthearted philosophy, there's no one in my life that I can imagine having sex with.

When I do take the leap, it's going to be a serious deal—a gesture of mutual respect, love, and commitment, even if it isn't the big *M* (marriage).

 Take a GanDer @

Deal with It! A Whole New Approach to Your Body, Brain, and Life as a Gurl, by Esther Drill, Heather McDonald, and Rebecca Odes
There are tons of *Our Bodies, Ourselves* kind of books out there, but *Deal with It!* is the coolest. Designed like something between *YM* magazine and a Warhol painting, the book deals frankly with everything from losing your virginity to body hair to self-mutilation. And it's chock-full of real girls' voices, too.

Changing Bodies, Changing Lives, by Ruth Bell
This is a great book for both genders that not only talks about body stuff, but also about life issues like gang violence. As in *Deal with It,* this books uses real teen voices wherever possible. That's what makes it cooler than most.

My fourteenth birthday

Chapter Six
Mental Health

Okay, so we all know our bodies go a little wacko during this time of life. We grow at grotesque rates, we get all hairy, and our secondary sex characteristics wake up and say, "Hello!"

But at least our minds are staying fairly with it during all this chaos, right?

Excuse me while I laugh really hard.

If anything, I think the worst part of my growing up has all been in my head.

Bursting into tears? Done that.

Mood swings? I've swooped around so much, I feel like an orangutan. I've gone from utter frustration to dark depressions to giggling highs, all in the course of one twenty-four-hour period.

And then there's that loss-of-perspective thing, where some small trauma gets stretched to epic tragedy: toilet paper on your shoe at school, he doesn't call, she does call. . . . You get the idea. But like, a week later, you can't even remember there was a catastrophe, much less what it was.

Our passions swoop out of control. Our parents fill us with contempt. We're racked with insecurity one moment, on top of the world the next. And on and on and on.

Take a Gander @

Crazy, by Benjamin Lebert, translated from German by Carol Brown Janeway Not only do I love this book because its author was sixteen when he wrote it, but it also expresses how most teenagers feel—a little crazy some of the time, abnormal most of the time, and in some way disabled much of the time. The novel follows a semiparalyzed, misfit boy to boarding school, where he finds true friends and perspective for the first time.

Stressed Out . . . .

Every day, most of us get up at the crack of dawn to make it to school on time, where we zip through a dizzying six or seven or even eight classes. (Have you had three major tests in one day? I have!) Then many of us head to our after-school jobs. Or we spend our time shuttling from one half of our divorced families to the other, or sitting in traffic as we rush from orthodontist to dermatologist to college application adviser. Don't even get me started on the homework.

On an almost daily basis, my life is this hectic. The same goes for most of my friends. Like, load up our Palm Pilots with extra RAM, 'cause we are booked.

This is the life I chose. If I wasn't simultaneously uploading

Goosehead's newest feature, writing a new *Whatever* Webisode, scheduling a press interview, and squeezing in homework and downtime with my buds, I wouldn't be nearly stimulated enough.

But stimulation comes at a cost. I have to learn to sleep at night knowing that the mortgage to my parents' house depends on a gamble—that Goosehead will eventually earn us a profit.

And I have to confront the fact that sometimes, it's humanly impossible for me to get everything done that I need to.

It doesn't really matter if my financial and professional responsibilities are huger than the average teen's. I still have the same worries. My fear of failing to make Goosehead's quarterly financial projections or scoring a television deal with my oh-so-charming pitch can be just as intense as your fear of the SATs. Both of those things affect our future, right?

If I think about life's high stakes too much, I freak, I freeze, I get totally paralyzed, unable to function at any one of my many tasks.

One solution is to cut down on all those tasks. If that's not possible, I give myself plenty of breathers to avoid blowing a fuse. I'll put the Mac on sleep and play some music, or I'll do a little just-for-fun surfing or call a friend who knows how to talk me down from the ledge. (If you don't have one of these important resources in your stable of buds, find one today! And

After a long day at the office . . .

be the 911 call for a pal of yours. It's your karmic duty.)

Another solution is to get some perspective. One look at a newspaper can remind me how foolish it is to freak about the dramas of my household, my high school, or even my job. In the grand scheme of things, I tell myself, this is nothing. That recognition doesn't make my crisis go away—but it does make me stop hyperventilating about it.

Does stress ever leave my life? Well, there are those rare moments that I find myself lazing on a Hawaiian beach (okay, this only happened once, during a vacation in 1998). Other than that? Not a chance—stress is my constant companion as I wend my way through my busy, busy life.

And as much as I complain that I should buy stock in Clinique under-eye cover-up, I don't really want a stress-free life. No stress means I'm not challenging myself, and not challenging myself means I'm not moving forward. And what's the point of that?

Weight of the World . . .

Of all the scary moments in my life, this one has got to top the charts—my meeting with Hank Cohen, an executive at MGM. This was the meeting in which Hank was going to decide whether or not to sign on *Whatever* and commit to selling our show to a TV network.

This meeting could change my life.

It could mean millions of dollars and a lot more responsibility.

And it was over dinner, so on top of everything else, I had to worry about slurping my soup.

Mark and I were heading to the restaurant. Mark was driving; I was trying to breathe.

"Ashley," Mark said, "there's a great line in the movie *Wall Street*: 'Life comes down to one or two big moments.' Well, this is one of those moments."

"Oh, my God."

"This is a big deal, Ash."

"I know," I answered.

"You know what you're going to say," Mark said.

I had my whole pitch memorized. I knew *Whatever* inside and out. It was my biggest passion.

And that's what got me through the meeting without flubbing, freaking, or flaking.

Once we started really rapping about *Whatever*, I forgot how huge Hank Cohen was and forgot to worry about splashing soup. Suddenly I was speaking as naturally as if I was chatting with a friend at school.

It worked. I nailed it, and Hank signed on to the project.

Express yourself completely— then keep quiet. Trust your natural responses and everything will fall into place.
—Tao De Ching

GolDeN Egg

The moral of this story? Enthusiasm trumps nervousness. Memorizing pitches and minding your table manners are all well and good. But caring deeply about something—whether it's a class report, a sports competition, or your after-school job—is the best recipe for success. Your passion is what's going to get you through those harrowing Big Moments.

Open Page in My Frustration Diary

Okay, you thought the "before" picture of me in Goosehead.com was scary? Check out this unadulterated excerpt (typos intact) from my journal on a very, very tough day.

Part of me looks at this rant and cringes. But another part feels triumphant—instead of venting at some hapless friend or relative or tearing my hair out, I instead took a time-out and wrote down this silent scream. (Okay, the music was blaring while I wrote it.) If you ask me, typing out your rage is (*a*) highly effective, (*b*) productive instead of destructive (who knows if you'll find some poetry in there later on?), and (*c*) hurtful to no one, except perhaps your keyboard.

I'm so frustrated and pissed. I don't even know what's going on. So much work . . . school has started!! I mean, at leadst during summer I don't answer my phone people are at camp . . . not too many temptations though there are a few. Now, it's like . . . "Are you going to the football game Friday?" "Are you going to Tom's party?" I'm like . . . no I have to work. . . which sucks a lot. Now, I'm sorry I'm fifteen . . . I think that way . . . I'm not capable at times to see the bigger picture. I'm trying though and so I'm fighting with myself. I hate this. There are times when I wish all I had to worry about was my makeup and which guy I like. My friends don't realize how lucky they are. Seriously. There are times when I am so unhappy. I feel so lonely it's terrible. I have all this love, so many people come to my site and it's like I still feel like I fall into these holes filled with one of the worst feelings that I would never wish on anyone. It's like . . . I was walking and a car hit me . . . outta nowhere. I don't know why . . . I just wasn't paying attention. I'm confused, sad, angry, depressed, and frusterated. With every person I talk to, with myself, with school, and with work. I wish I had a punching bag to kill, In fact I think I might go to the gym later.

Limp Bizkit say it well: "It's just one of those days when you don't want to wake up, everything is #%!&^*, everybody sucks, you don't really know why, but you wanna justify rippin someone's head off. No human contact and if you interact your life is on contract. Your best bet is to stay away mother f***er, it's just one of those days!"

Okay, so now I'm bustin out some Eminem in my fit of anger, God if that phone rings once more I swear I'll throw it out the window.

When I feel depressed, disappointed, or just out of sorts, I throw myself a Pity Party. There's usually plenty of junk food involved, but the main event is the movie. My all-time favorite PP movies, the ones that make me cry every time, are . . .

• *Singles:* This Cameron Crowe movie is such a quirky look at the dating life. I love how vulnerable and real the characters are. And of course, I love the mushy, happy ending. Sigh . . .
• *Jerry Maguire:* What can I say? Cameron Crowe has me at hello.
• *High Fidelity:* I love the music. I love the acting. Most of all, I love the brilliant writing in this movie, which is based on a great book by Nick Hornby.
• *City of Angels:* Oh, the end just kills me every time!

Even if you're on the right track, you'll get run over if you just sit there.
—Will Rogers

GolDeN Egg

Taking a Time-out . . .
Here are little things I try to do for myself when I need a little TLC . . .

- Take a walk to think
- Write in my journal or read
- Call a long-distance touch-stone pal like Arelyn or Whitney
- Work out
- Watch a brainless TV show for a half hour
- Dance around my room and sing loudly along with the CD player (when nobody else is home, of course!)
- Page my best friend and get me to the nearest diner for therapeutic conversation and coffee

GolDeN Egg

Suicide

Suicide

Technically, my sister Whitney is a step—she's my stepmom, Melanie's, daughter from her first marriage. But Whitney's only a year younger than I am and such a good friend, I don't ever qualify our relationship. We're sisters, case closed.

That's why I was both not surprised, and totally confused, when Whitney tried to commit suicide about a year ago.

Whitney was always the kid in our family who clamored for attention. She was the one who acted out and threw tantrums and insisted, for instance, that she would not wear that puffy, fluffy dress to church. I was the good girl, who clamped her lips shut and put on the hateful dress rather than cause a scene.

I was outgoing and made friends easily. Whitney was always a little wistful, standing on the sidelines, looking in. She felt a little lost, living in a big family with four younger siblings. It was attention she was looking for the first time she swallowed a bunch of pills.

She called me the day she did it, practically blowing up my pager and cell phone. I was at school at the time. When I finally reached her, she told me what she'd done.

It was one of the scariest things I've ever heard.

But once I knew Whitney was safe, I have to admit, I was pissed.

"How selfish of you," I said. "Do you think no one would care if you killed yourself?"

"You're the only person who would," she said.

I convinced her of how much her family and friends in Missouri care about her and insisted that she call me whenever she needed someone to remind her of what she has to live for.

That's why I was shocked when a few months later, Whitney tried again, swallowing a handful of Tylenol. This time, she was institutionalized for three days after her stomach was pumped. I think staying in the hospital terrified her more than the vague idea of death ever did.

The truth is, Whitney did this for a reason. A friend had told her—swallow some pills, they'll pump your stomach, it'll all be over, and then they'll pay attention.

That doesn't make her suicide attempt less serious, or less sad.

Reading the Goosehead bulletin boards, I hear about kids in horrible situations. They're abused or neglected or taken advantage of by friends or lovers. They're making huge decisions about abortion. Or they're living with an alcoholic parent or battling addiction themselves.

This was one of the first times one of those "issues" hit home for me. I had dealt with it once before when I was younger, but it was never quite as close.

Mark's older sister committed suicide, and I remember watching how our family responded to it, especially Mark. He said he understood but at the same time felt angry over what she had done. This was the first time that I saw Mark really break down. I remember thinking that he hadn't really cried or anything over his sister. Then there was a knock at the door—Doug, Mark's best friend, came to check on Mark. They never said a word to each other. Mark just started to cry, and Doug just put his arms around him. I went back to my room and told my mom that Mark was crying. She went out to check on him, I followed her, and when she saw Doug, she just took me by the hand and led me back to my bedroom. I knew how much Mark loved his sister and that it would probably really hurt me if something like that ever happened.

Then just a few years later, I was feeling overwhelmed by the same type of situation. After all the affirmations I gave Whitney and all the hours we talked when she attempted suicide the first time, she still tried again.

Now she's getting professional help, which is reassuring. But there are no guarantees. I have to recognize that there's only so much I can do to help Whitney. I've let her know how much I love her and how lost I'd be if she left this world, and I've tried to help her love herself.

But the rest is up to her.

I think her experience has given both of us a major reality check. Life is tough, and it's not getting any easier. Checking out might cross your mind. It might even tempt you. But it's no solution. It's senseless destruction. It will hurt your friends and family more than you can imagine, and worst of all, it's shutting the door on all your possibilities.

What a tragedy that would be.

 Take a Gander @

If you or someone you know is having a problem, don't be afraid to ask for help:

Suicide help: www.sfsuicide.org/index2.html

Helps teens on the streets: www.child.net/street.htm

Helps keep kids safe: www.child.net/violence.htm

National Runaway Hotline: 800-621-4000

National Hotline for Missing & Exploited Children: 800-843-5678
Youth Crisis Hotline: 800-448-4663

Confession—the first time I ever got a C, I cried. It looked so ugly on my report card that I couldn't stand it. My parents didn't bother to ground me for letting my grades drop. I punished myself enough on my own.

I'm a perfectionist—a classic case.

I used to hatch plots to clean my room from top to bottom without being asked. I would grin with satisfaction, imagining not only the spotlessness of my room, but also my parents' exclamations of surprise and joy.

But sometimes my mom beat me to the punch, casually saying, "Can you clean your room up later?"

"Why'd you have to say that?" I would wail. "I was gonna clean it anyway. Now it's not going to be as good!"

Today I'm hopefully less dorky than that. But perfectionism still courses through my veins. This is great for my work ethic. I always keep at a task until it's done right, not just until I get tired of it.

But the problem with being a perfectionist is, well, you want everything to be perfect. And perfection? It's a total fantasy.

That's why I sometimes downplay my achievements. I think, in the back of my mind, I feel that once I've achieved something, it becomes less huge, less exciting.

Take the first time I saw an article written about me and Goosehead.com. I was totally psyched! I told all my friends about it and felt giddy every time I looked at it. After the glamour wore off, though, I took a closer look. That's not really the BEST picture of me, is it? I thought. And I was misquoted. And this is just the local paper, not a national magazine or anything—big whoop.

After that, every press mention was less exciting than the one before. I could always find some fault with it.

One time my mom resorted to coming into my room and thrusting a magazine in my face.

"Look at this, you're in *US Weekly*," she announced. "Did you see this?"

"I saw it," I replied blandly.

"No, I don't think you really did," she sputtered, "This is a big deal. You should be proud of yourself!"

She's right. I have a hard time saying to myself, "Good job, Ashley!" When someone gives me constructive criticism, I tend to edit out their praise and hear only the negatives.

I'm trying to get over this attitude. I make an effort to catch myself in the act of dissing my own accomplishments. One thing that's helped, strangely enough, is my recently falling grades in school.

After Goosehead took off, my GPA began to go into a small but steady decline. My teachers started showing signs of distress. But for once, I didn't. (Okay, I know this isn't a very role model-y thing to admit to, but it's the truth. . . .)

I saw my less-than-perfect grades as a worthy compromise for Goosehead's success. I realized, You know what? I can't do it all. And my best work is not always an A. The most important thing is to work as hard as I can and do my best, no matter what the outcome.

In other words, I think I've taken the first step toward cutting myself a break every once in a while!

 ## Take a Gander @

Don't Sweat the Small Stuff for Teens: Simple Ways to Keep Your Cool in Stressful Times, **by Richard Carlson, Ph.D.**
Okay, there's no getting around the fact that Richard Carlson can sometimes write with an, ahem, parental tone of voice. But look beyond occasional fits of dorkiness, and his brief bits of advice can be really priceless. He reminds me of things I believe but easily lose sight of over the course of my busy life, stuff like, "let people talk" and "make space in your heart for those really bad days."

Being "Mom" . . .

When I played basketball in junior high, my team's nickname for me was "Mom." That's because, like any good mom, I was always tending to my buds' bruises and hurt feelings before I stopped to consider whether I was okay.

Even though I've given up b-ball, my Mom role lives on.

Sometimes, in my effort to take care of all my friends, I totally neglect myself. I might whirl through a day, applying a Band-Aid where needed and listening understandingly. Not until I collapse into bed that night might I realize, "Hey, I'm totally bummed about such and such."

By then, it's too late to call a friend or deal on my own. I can only wring my hands in an insomniac haze.

I love my caretaker role and don't ever want to give it up. But I also know if I don't take care of my emotional needs, nobody else will do it for me.

So, I've been trying to create some balance (another one of those over-used but oh-so-apt buzzwords) in my life, making sure I get a word in edgewise when my friends and I have heart-to-hearts and making sure I deal with my problems.

And when balance isn't an option, I go for my more drastic, but oh-so-effective twenty-four-hour cure. . . .

Mental-Health Days

As anyone who's been through finals or the SATs or some other concentrated stretch of work knows, life's pressures don't dissipate each night when you go to sleep. Instead, they sometimes seem to build and build and build. Taking a half-hour break just doesn't help.

When I'm, say, crying at midnight because I've been working on math homework for hours and still don't get it, I know it's time for a mental health day.

I'll pick a day. I'll clear the day of all commitments, even if it hurts a little to do it. I mean, what's more important? Yet another mall jaunt with my friends, or my sanity? When I've carved out some blissfully empty hours for myself, I'll spend that time letting off steam, healing my burns and bruises, and relaxing.

So what I do? All my favorite things.

I'll usually sleep in and spend the day in my pj's. There's some movie watching and plenty of dancing and singing along to the CD player (when my parents are at work, of course). I'll read and write in my journal. Geek that I am, mental-health days have to include some productive activity, too. I'll try to catch up or even work ahead on schoolwork to make the upcoming days less stressful.

Just as pressure builds up, so do the feel-good vibes from a mental health day. Taking that time to focus on myself can propel me for weeks. Which definitely makes it a worthy investment.

Chapter Seven
The Big Picture

I had a wake-up call a while back, when I was doing a chat on ABC.com to follow up a Goosehead segment that had aired on PrimeTime Thursday. Most of the people popping questions into the chat room were adults, and a lot of them were all, "Do you think *Whatever* promotes materialism?"

The implication was clear. These folks thought Goosehead was merely about fun and games—an escape from the real world. Which it is! But it's also much more.

On Goosehead chats and bulletin boards, kids are talking about some serious stuff, everything from parental consent for abortion to the environment to politics, even though most of us hanging at the site aren't old enough to vote yet.

This comes as a surprise to many adults. Important issues and teenagers mix as easily as Israel and the PLO in their minds.

Am I going to get pissed off about this injustice? No way. I'll merely prove them wrong.

My head is filled with a lot more than the latest M•A•C colors and the newest Ryan Phillippe movie. And I know I'm not alone. I've met kids who pound the pavement, collecting signatures for Amnesty International and Greenpeace. They're spending their spring breaks hammering for Habitat for Humanity. They're tutoring after school or studying to get into prelaw programs. They're changing the world—or getting ready to.

And we're all talking, talking, talking, forming beliefs and philosophies that will steady us as we forge ahead.

Remember all those opinions I talked about in this book's introduction? Well, brace yourselves, buds, 'cause here they come. . . .

School

School comes first because it dominates our days. We memorize the Pythagorean theorem and learn about the discovery of DNA and who shot the shot heard round the world. We take tests and score our As. And then we forget these bits of knowledge faster than you can say, "I've got a date on Friday night."

My mom and I recently had a talk about this school matter. She said she thought we students were forced to go to high school only to teach us how to balance life in the "real world." In high school you have friends, homework, tests, boyfriends or girlfriends, projects, parties, family, etc. When you get out of college and begin a career, you have deadlines, a boss, coworkers, relationships, family, your own home, bills, etc. There's nothing we learn in school aside from balancing and socializing that we couldn't learn in a library or by watching the Discovery Channel.

I'm not saying it's not important to learn the basics. If we don't learn history, we're doomed to repeat it. Without the writing we do in English and speech classes, we'd never learn to think analytically. Chemistry and physics help us understand the world in which we live. And algebra—okay, I'm stumped; I have no idea what algebra is good for.

Truth be told, a lot of us are just getting through our classes so we can hang with our friends in the halls and make it to college; that is, real life.

But why not experience and learn about real life in high school? My favorite classes have been world cultures and mock trial, in which students had to play lawyers, build a case, and then present it in front of an actual judge. But these were just tastes of the outside world. I crave even more applicable knowledge. Our parents are all obsessed with the stock market, for instance. Let's learn about that in school. What about venture capitalism and 80/20 business models and entrepreneurship?

I want to learn the things that I had to learn on my own as soon as I started a company. That's what should be taught in school.

"WHATEVER"

Feeling listless about school? Totally unmotivated? I've discovered a way to spike your learning curve and get seriously interested in the whole school thing—form a good relationship, maybe even a friendship, with a cool teacher.

My favorite teacher in ninth grade was my speech and theater teacher, Robert DiMuro, otherwise known as Coach D. In Coach D's class we spent time having heated discussions about issues and then wrote speeches about them.

I'd often finish my work early and use the extra time to hang with Coach D. It was so refreshing to talk to a teacher who (a) took his students seriously and (b) had interesting ideas to talk about himself! Our conversations were usually brief, but they were enough to make me look forward to going to Coach D's class every day. They also made me much more interested in what we were learning.

If, by chance, there are some hip teachers at your school, I urge you to engage them in conversation and get to know them. (Look closely— a lot of teachers are cooler than they appear!) It'll change the way you think about class.

Media
Media

Okay, I create content for the Web and TV, I get press in magazines, newspapers and Web sites, and, of course, I've published a book. Naturally, I think about the media a lot.

But I think I would be fascinated by pop culture even if I weren't a part of it. Because, face it, the media is everywhere.

Our generation has a different take on this fact than a lot of older folks. I mean, in the scarily recent past, there were only four networks on television and no cable. Pre-MTV (which is also, as it happens, pre-me), film and television moved much more slowly. There were no half-second cuts, warp-speed video games, or split-screen movies. Back then, you sometimes had to wait an entire day to get your news. Today you only have to point and click at ten-thirty to hear about something that happened at ten-fifteen.

Maybe all this hyperstimulating media is the cause of ADD. Maybe it's destroyed our ability to digest a good book. Maybe violent music influences kids to shoot up their high schools. Maybe skinny fashion models encourage young girls to starve themselves to death.

I honestly can't say whether any of these things are true or false. (And with all the conflicting research bouncing around, I don't think the experts can, either.) But here's what I think, or at least, what I hope . . .

As the media saturate our lives, I think we kids are the ones best equipped to handle it. We practically emerged from the womb as sophisticated consumers. We don't know a world without 150 channels or a zillion potential hits on the Internet. So, we don't get bogged down and overwhelmed with all the media's bounty. Instead we tailor our consumption to our wonderfully unique selves.

For girls who loathe looking at glossies full of skinny models, there are real-girl mags and Web sites that are just as cool as those in the mainstream.

Kids looking for tunes that won't make their parents wig are exploring Christian rock or alternative music.

And anyone feeling alienated because there's no magazine devoted to his oh-so-obscure passion for baking with wheat grass can check a few search engines or cable-access channels. I'm sure he'll find others like himself.

If there's really nothing out there that suits us, well, we just turn around and create our own Goosehead.coms. I may be one of the bigger teenage mavens on the Web, but I know I'm not the only one.

Here's my point. Media can control you, making you buy stuff you don't really want, making you hate what you see in the mirror, and filling your head with negative energy. *Or* . . . you can take the reins. You can see the media the way I do—as an opportunity to find a community and make your voice heard.

The million-dollar question that's on every parent's mind is, Is the media bad? Is it warping our kids' minds?

I think the answer is in our hands (Regis, that is my final answer!). It's up to us whether the media is inflicted upon us or is something we control as smart, cool consumers.

Religion . . .

My dad and his family are strict Mormons. We're talking church every

Sunday. So when I lived with them in Utah, which is the capital of Mormon America and a very devout community, I went to church every Sunday, too. I learned all about the Mormons' lifestyle and their vision of God.

My mom and Mark are not Mormons. They have their own beliefs in God. But I do go to a Catholic school that makes religion a daily presence in my life.

Actually, I'm glad I go to my school. Not only do we do the Catholic thing, but we also take religion class, where we learn about Buddhism, Islam, and a ton of other traditions. Learning about all these religions is helping me figure out what might work for me. At the very least, it helps me understand people who come from different backgrounds. Since religious identity can be so divisive, I think that understanding is a valuable gift.

My views on religion are constantly changing. Just because I'm not into the organized-religion thing now doesn't mean I won't be someday. I don't have everything figured out, and my spiritual house is far from orderly. That's as it should be, I think. I'm only sixteen. I'm just at the beginning of this journey.

Ageism . . .

I'm always wary when Mark and I meet with a new, adult business contact because every once in a while, I get what I called the family-programming treatment.

This contact will talk to Mark in a serious, confident tone of voice. He'll use vocabulary straight out of **The New York Times**. It's a conversation between equals. Think **Law and Order**.

And then he'll turn to me and start speaking more slowly and simply. He'll dumb things down. He'll humor me. He'll treat me like a kid. Think *Barney.*

Big mistake.

When someone treats me with such indignity, I turn the tables right back on him and clam up. I can't act like an equal with someone who doesn't treat me as one. It goes against everything that I believe in and everything that Goosehead is about! Then to their surprise, when they contact Mark later for some sort of business dealings, he says that we're not interested. They ask, Why? Mark basically says because "Ashley's not interested." Oops! Guess what? I make decisions, too.

I'm not saying that I'm some sort of superteen, wise beyond her years, a total intellectual freak. No, I'm as normal as the next kid. And I know nothing can replace, say, thirty years of experience or a college degree.

But the fact that I'm young doesn't mean I'm inferior. And if I have the responsibilities of someone twice my age—and face it, I do—I should be treated with respect.

My parents, bless 'em, totally get this.

"Ash," they say, "if you act sixteen, we're going to treat you like you're sixteen." That means curfews, homework monitoring, restricted phone time, etc.

But I don't act sixteen. I live up to my responsibilities, whether it's a homework assignment or a professional deadline. I keep track of

HONK!!!

Why Is It That . . .

- **We're old enough to have to pay full price at a movie theater but not old enough to see an R-rated movie?**
- **We're old enough to hold jobs; that is, pay taxes, but we don't get to vote?**
- **The government will allow us to fight in a war, maybe even die, defending the country at eighteen, but won't let us drink legally until we're twenty-one?**
- **Prosecutors are so quick to try fourteen-year-old criminals as adults, but they won't give adult privileges to teenagers who do precociously good things?**

my own schedule and make sure I get to where I need to go. I baby-sit. I drive.

Nevertheless, to adults who don't get it, I am a little kid until I reach that magical eighteenth birthday.

This makes no sense to me. The late teen years are totally unique. They're the last gasp of childhood and first breath of adulthood. If we're not voter-registration-card-carrying grown-ups, we're definitely not little kids anymore. And adults need to get with the program.

My hope is that the prominence of Goosehead.com and other teen-created businesses—whether they're nonprofit service projects or some rad clothing line—will give all teenagers more of the respect we deserve.

This doesn't mean you have to start stalking around in a pinstriped suit and ignoring your urges to watch *Charmed*. Be yourself—have fun. Do that teenage mall—movie—burger and fries thing. But do it responsibly, and use some of your time to do something productive. Eventually most grown-ups are going to stand up and take notice.

No matter how much I value the grown-up parts of my life, I recognize that one of my strongest creative assets is my youth. It's important not to lose that sense of joy and wonder that comes from being a kid—ever. This quote always helps me remember that. . . .

How to be an artist: Stay loose. Learn to watch snails. Plant impossible gardens. Invite someone dangerous to tea. Make little signs that say "yes!" and post them around your house. Make friends with freedom and uncertainty. Look forward to dreams. Cry during movies. Swing as high as you can on a swingset by moonlight. Cultivate moods. Refuse to "Be responsible." Do it for love. Take lots of naps. Give money away.
Do it now. The money will follow. Believe in magic. Laugh a lot. Celebrate every gorgeous moment. Take moon-baths. Have wild imaginings, transformative dreams, and perfect calm. Draw on the walls. Read every day. Imagine yourself magic. Giggle with children. Listen to old people. Open up. Dive in. Be free. Bless yourself. Drive away fear. Play with everything. Entertain your inner child. You are innocent. Build a fort with blankets. Get wet. Hug trees. Write love letters.

—Sark, 1989

GolDeN Egg

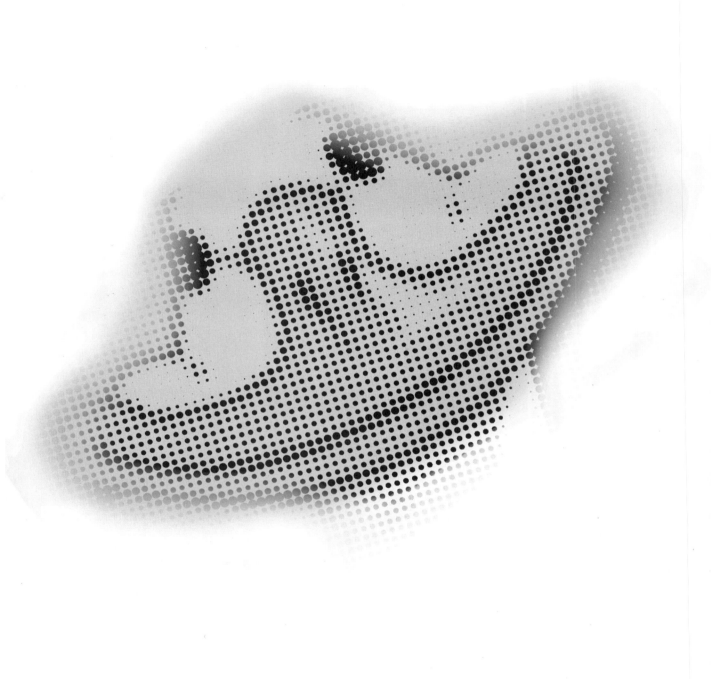

Chapter Eight
Where I've Been and
Where I'm Going

It would be impossible to list all the changes that have happened in my life since I started Goosehead.com. But many of them—like my transition from homepage administrator to company CEO—have been so gradual that they've been easy to get used to.

Then there've been the quick changes. One minute I was a kid who'd been written up in a couple of local newspapers. The next I was splashed all over the media, from the *Roseanne* show to *PrimeTime Live*, from

What lies behind us and what lies before us are tiny matters compared to what lies within us. —Ralph Waldo Emerson

GolDeN Egg

The New York Times to *People* and *Entertainment Weekly* magazine.

It took almost no time for people to start coming up to me to say, "Hey, you're that Web girl!" Or even, "Are you Ashley Power?"

When you grow up in Los Angeles, seeing celebrities is not as earth-shaking as it might be in other parts of the country. And growing up in my house, you might find celebrities hanging around the house! My mom and Mark have always had friends "in the business"—some are dolly grips and some are movie stars. But in my parents' minds, they're all the same. In mine, too. I mean, why does being famous make you somehow more interesting or worthy? The famous people I've met have been totally . . . normal. Meeting them is like running into someone that you recognize on the street.

It's exciting to talk to someone who's done amazing work, but for me, the fact that they're famous doesn't really add to that.

The appeal of fame has become even more mysterious since I started doing the paparazzi thing.

When the people who recognize me congratulate me on my work, it's really cool. But sometimes they look at me like I'm an alien or a freak of nature! We're talking megascrutiny.

When you're famous, not only are people examining your clothes, your hair, and the state of your complexion everywhere you go (see my rant on page 65), they're also watching your every move. At least, that's how it can feel sometimes. The role-model thing is not for me. I make mistakes, sometimes have bad judgments, and

Everyone seems to have a clear idea of how other people should lead their lives, but none about his or her own.
—Paulo Coelho, in *The Alchemist*

Go1DeN Egg

occasionally flub a test in school. I fight with my parents and get irritated at my brother, and as anyone who watches *Whatever* might know, I've been grounded for forgetting to scoop up dog poop.

Putting me on a pedestal is saying I'm perfect or ought to be. And that's not what I am.

If reading this book does anything, I hope it convinces people that fame is just a condition of a job. It's not something that makes you prettier, better, or even more interesting than the nonfamous kid next door.

Remember this the next time you have the urge to stop and stare, and point, and whisper at some celeb that you pass on the street.

Dealing with Dad . . .

A lot of things have happened in the past. Some I don't understand. Some I wish were different. And some I accept. Divorce is not like breaking up with a boyfriend or girlfriend. There's money, possessions, and sometimes even children involved. I am a kid with divorced parents. I can't remember or imagine my parents in the same room together, let alone enjoying each other's company. But there are lots of things I do remember and lots of things I still deal with today because they are no longer married.

A recent surprise visit to see my dad

When I was five years old, I asked my mom if I was the cause of my parents' divorce. She told me that her divorce had nothing to do with me—things just weren't working out. I wasn't convinced. I think most kids of divorced parents take a long time to realize that they are not at fault. The relationship that I remember my parents having was screaming at each other on the phone. I cried myself to sleep some nights as I listened to my mom yelling at my dad on the other end of the phone. I was confused. What were they fighting about? Why couldn't she leave him alone? And I thought somehow it was all my fault. If only I was a better kid. I couldn't help but wonder, if I hadn't been born, would they have been together longer?

As I grew older the screaming continued, as did my tears and confusion. Then, when someone new enters your divorced parents' lives (like a new boyfriend/girlfriend), it gets even more complicated. Every kid whose parents are divorced fantasizes about their parents getting back together and everything being perfect and happy. But when a new relationship begins to flourish, your fantasies are ruined and you develop a lot of resentment toward the new person in your parent's life.

When this happened in my life, almost simultaneously for both my mom and dad, it was a double whammy of resentment that seemed way too much for a little kid to handle. I felt like I was the only kid out there that had ever gone through something like this! I felt like I had nowhere

Dream as if you'll live forever. Live as if you'll die tomorrow.
—James Dean

GolDeN Egg

to turn. I kept it all inside and was feeling desperate for everything to be normal.

My mom took me to a family counselor to talk about my feelings. Boy, was it a load off my back to realize that my feelings and my anger were completely normal and somewhat healthy. Talking about your feelings is so important—so many people think that feelings are bad. But the truth is, feelings are just feelings; they aren't good or bad. Everyone has them—it's your actions and reactions based on feelings that could be bad. So talking about how you feel is good; it can help you through a tough time without having to "act out" in a negative way.

Things got tough when my dad moved away from California. That meant I had to fly alone on a plane and visit him and his new family for sometimes weeks at a time. It kind of sucks getting on a plane on Christmas Day, when all you want to do is be at home and play with all the cool stuff you just got for Christmas. Because of having to travel on a plane to another state, my visits weren't very regular, so when I did visit my dad, it didn't seem like "home" to me. Sure, my dad was there,

When it comes down to it, we all just want to be loved. —John Lennon

Golden Egg

but I was in unfamiliar surroundings in a house where I didn't have my own stuff or any of my friends. That was tough. The little things mattered, like not knowing where the cups were or where the towels were or not knowing the neighborhood kids. I sometimes felt like I threw things off balance when I visited dad. The family was used to me *not* being there, and then I'd come and everything was different for them, too. I know my dad loves me more than I sometimes believe, and he tells me every time I visit, "Now the *entire* family is together." But when I was young, my insecurities bit at me like mosquitoes.

Since I live with my mom, I see her every day. She's around and observes everything from my hyper days, my grumpy days, my predate preparation, to my after-school gossip. She knows my friends' voices when they call, and I point out the new guys I like when she picks me up from school. Dad can't be there for all those times. I wish he could be because it's hard to explain all those little nuances over the phone; sometimes you just "had to be there."

I know my dad loves me more than anything, and even though we may fight or disagree sometimes, I love him, too. I feel really fortunate that both my parents give me unconditional love and let me know that I am special—only that can get me through some of the tough times. It lets me know that I have two people behind me, full of faith and love, that I can always turn to.

Keep on Honkin' . . .

Keep on Honkin' . . .

Whatever is growing. It's an incredibly exciting success. But while someday people might think of *Whatever* as that teen show on TV, it will always be linked in my mind to Goosehead.com. My favorite episodes will always be the ones we shot all over our house in Burbank with a totally tight budget, friends as extras, and props scrounged from Josh's toy chest. (Remember the baby-doll episode? It was the best!)

I'll always have fond memories of Goosehead's early shoestring days, too, when it took me weeks to put a new page up on the site and I was fighting my way onto search engines.

As anyone who's visited Goosehead lately knows, it's becoming way slick. We've finally established our core site, and now we can go back and fill in the blanks. We're doing all the fun and crazy stuff I used to dream about but never had the resources for.

Among recent additions to Goosehead are . . .

- T. J. Espinoza's weekly dance step tutorial, featuring moves T. J. picked up on tour with Britney Spears. (There are plenty of pics of T. J. backstage with the great blond one, too.)
- Dan Habib's photographic series about teen sexuality. This serious documentary is gritty and gripping and real.
- Our new makeup and hair page that my friend Kristin is spearheading.

- A fashion page, complete with Goosehead duds for sale.
- Airing celebrity interview chats that I have been doing on the site.

And there's always more coming!

This is the time that Webmasters live for. Goosehead has a nice-sized budget, name recognition, and more than 300,000 hits per day. I'm thrilled! I'm also feeling the pressure. More viewers means more disparate people to please, more criticism, more scrutiny, and more opportunities to mess up.

But I've found that the occasional mess-up—offending someone or stepping over the boundaries of taste—is a good thing. In my opinion, if you don't make a mistake every once in a while, you're not taking enough creative risks.

Someday I know I'll have to take the ultimate risk and hand Goosehead over to someone else. After all, I'm not going to be a teenager forever, and I do have other goals to pursue, like going to college and becoming a film director.

Still, Goosehead will always feel like my baby. I'll never take it for granted, and I'll never completely abandon it, either. No matter how slick the site gets or how old I get(!), I'll always have my CEO's two cents to offer.

I look forward to mentoring and molding some brilliant new "face of Goosehead" and watching him or her take the reins and run with them. But until then, I'll keep pushing the site onward and upward myself.

Who knows exactly what's next for Goosehead? As much as I run the site, I feel it belongs to the viewers, who are very vocal about their opinions. Maybe they'll demand more Goosehead TV or turn the site into a big cult chat room. Maybe it'll become a fashion 'zine or a poetry scene.

What do I want for Goosehead? You should know by now. Whatever! Anything and everything. I guess all I can say is, Stay tuned!

To laugh often and much; to win the respect of intelligent people and the affection of children; to earn the appreciation of honest critics and endure the betrayal of false friends; to appreciate beauty, to find the best in others; to leave the world a bit better, whether by a healthy child, a garden, or a redeemed social condition; to know even one life has breathed easier because you have lived. This is to have succeeded.

—Ralph Waldo Emerson

GolDeN Egg

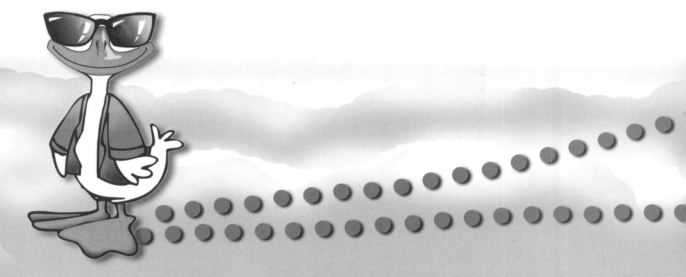

Be Your Own
Webmaster:
Everything You
Need to Know

Be Your Own
Webmaster:
Everything You
Need to Know

Be Your Own
Webmaster

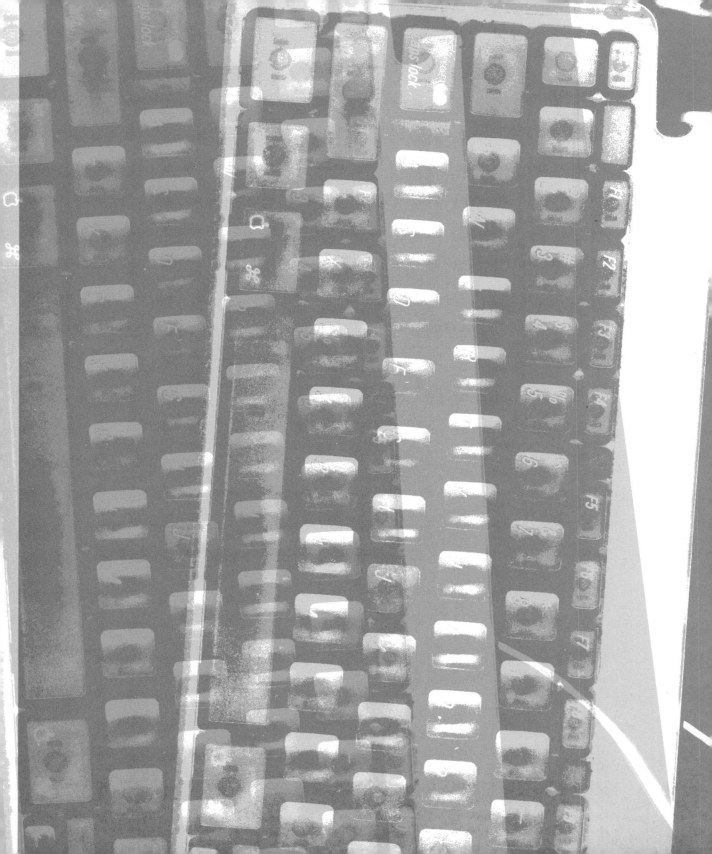

Chapter Nine
Building Your Web Page

Pop quiz! What geeky, Web head stereotype most pisses me off?

a) We all wear high-water khakis and nerdy,
   Woody Allen eyewear.
b) We have no lives outside our computers.
c) We are mouth breathers.
d) We don't speak English; we speak Code,
   a language so complex and confounding, no
   normal person could understand it.

Well, I'm quite fond of my khaki capris and funky black glasses, thank you very much. And if you want to insist that all Web heads are obsessive geeks, hey, be my guest. Hope you're enjoying it back there in 1997!

Which is to say, the correct answer is . . . *(d).*

Many people are way intimidated by *HTML* (hypertext markup language—the code in which all things Web are written). They think of creating a Web site as completely out of their league.

Take it from me, a self-taught Webmaster—that is so not the case. Anybody can build a Web page. Especially when Web-writing programs are being refined and updated all the time.

Take a Gander @

An interactive html tutorial for beginners:
www.davesite.com/webstation/html

In fact, that's one of the coolest things about the Web—it's always changing. It's like a big, constantly growing plant. Everyone who tends to this plant can change the way it grows. One person adds a little water, another person throws in some plant food, a third moves it from the sun to the shade . . . and *wham*, suddenly the plant has grown an extra vine or changed colors ever so slightly.

Anyone can make a major impact on the Web, not just big corporations or sites with tons of advertising dollars. Shawn Fanning, who invented Napster, proved that. I'm sure back when he was pumping out code for his tunage downloading system, he never dreamed he'd be called before Congress for upsetting the balance of copyright law.

Just as I never dreamed, when I was slaving over my little home page at age thirteen, that it would one day become Goosehead.com, a three-hundred-thousand-hits-per-day teen community.

And who knows—maybe you and your PC are brewing up the next Napster or Goosehead. One day you're sitting in your room, thinking, "Hey, I've got a cool idea." Next thing you know, you're grounded for life.

But you'll also have achieved instantaneous cult fame for revolutioniz-ing the Web. Web culture moves so fast, I swear, there are about two revolutions a year. So get ready—the next guru could be you.

But first, you've got to create your bitchin' site. How do you start? Following is all your primary, need-to-know stuff.

I won't go into every little detail, say, comparing and contrasting *GIFs*, *PNGs*, and *JPEGs* (these are all different formats in which photos can be uploaded onto a Web site). Please—all that stuff could fill another book entirely.

But I will tell you the basic steps you'll need to create your own site and what resources you can go to when it's time to sweat the small stuff. . . .

HTML . . .

As I've mentioned, *hypertext markup language* is the language of the Internet's World Wide Web. Rather than words, the language is code. And this code allows you to fill up a screen with text, pictures, and graphic design to create a fabulous product, one that's like a TV show, a magazine page, and a telephone conversation all rolled into one.

The best part is, although HTML is a Web language, it can be manipulated in files on your hard drive. So you can create Web pages on your own computer, be it IBM, Mac, UNIX, whatever.

There are purists who say the only way to really wrap your brain around Web design is to learn HTML inside and out, then write up your code yourself. We're talking stuff that looks more confusing than the worst trigonometry equation, like . . . (CSAg = window.navigator.userAgent; CSBVers = parseInt(CSAg.charAt(CSAg.indexOf("/")+1),10); function IsIE() {return CSAg.indexOf("MSIE")>0;}.

Then there are those who say—hey, there are a ton of programs out there that write HTML code for you. Why waste hours sweating over the drawing board?

Speaking as one who got her start handwriting my HTML, I am so in the latter camp. Because you know what? I don't care what all that gob-bledygook means as long as my Web page works.

If you choose to take the easy way out, here are my favorite HTML-writing programs, otherwise known as editors:

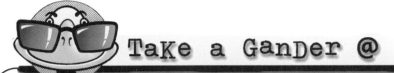

Take a GanDer @

Adobe GoLive is the program I use. It's awesome, mostly because it has a great interface with Adobe Photoshop, which is the program I use to create all my graphics for Goosehead. (I'll discuss Photoshop later.)
You can download a free trial of GoLive at **www.adobe.com**.

Microsoft's Frontpage 2000 is another popular program. Find out more about it at **www.microsoft.com/frontpage**.

HTML isn't the only code out there. There are other languages that you may have heard about, like *Java*, *C++*, *Perl*, and *Flash*, which is used to create animation. But I don't recommend that newbies get into these languages before they've completely mastered HTML. That's like trying to parallel park before you've figured out how to drive in a straight line. In other words, premature and totally overwhelming.

Put Java scripts in your future plans, but for now, it's best to be basic and stick with good ol' HTML.

Learning the Ropes . . .

Now that you've got your editor, you have to learn how to use it. Most of these programs provide templates to work with—they're sort of like grids on which you can assemble your code like a puzzle.

There are also a ton of tutorials on the Web. The best way to find a good one for you is to go to a search engine (try Goosehead's!) and type in a program name, such as Adobe GoLive. You'll find a stockpile of tutorials from which to choose. Log in and the program will prompt you from there.

You might also try a book like *The Internet for Dummies* (I know this series is lame, but they really do give good step-by-step instructions) or a videotape. I bought a VHS tape from www.Lynda.com that explained how to use GoLive in easy terms. I was able to rewind the tape and watch it over and over again until all the concepts were etched in my mind.

This is the stage that requires the most patience. Learning to build a Web page is like learning to ski. It's a foreign concept to grasp, but once you get over your initial fear and confusion and get it, Web design quickly becomes second nature.

Once this happens, you can buckle down and start writing your own page using your editor.

Take a Gander @

Links that can help you learn the basics of Web site building . . .

- *Goosehead tutorial:*
  www.goosehead.com/goosevillage/help/index.html: Go here to have me walk you gently through the steps of building your first Web site.

- *Netmaking:*
  www.netmaking.com: This site's motto is, "Dedicated to Helping Webmasters Make Better Web Sites." These folks will teach you how to create, maintain, and improve your Web site with free articles, tutorials, scripts, and site reviews.

- *Developer Center:*
  www.webmastersland.com/devcenter: This tutorial site has over forty Adobe Photoshop tutorials, along with primers for JavaScript, Macromedia Flash, and many more.

A Valuable Shortcut . . .

I read an article recently in which a novelist recalled a summer job he'd once had at a publishing house. He was a total grunt, nothing more than a typist. But lucky for him, one of the manuscripts he was given to transcribe was a handwritten novel by Ernest Hemingway! He said typing this great author's words taught him more about writing than he could have imagined.

That's sort of how I feel about lifting code from other Web sites. It's a great way to get your legs when you're a newbie. You can learn how code is written from experienced Webmasters and then modify the code to make it your own.

How do you do this? First, find a Web site you really like. When you see something in a page you want to use, go to the tool bar in your browser (*Netscape Navigator* or *Internet Explorer*). Go to the *View* label and drag down to *source code* or *page source*. Suddenly the pictures and text will disappear, and you'll see the page in HTML, as the Webmaster wrote it!

Then you can simply copy the code you like into your own Web page template and futz with it until it becomes uniquely yours.

Again, purists are going to frown on this method, but I say, imitation is the best flattery! Accessing the wisdom of Web pioneers who came before you is paying them homage, not dissing them!

Design . . .

Designing the page is my favorite part of being a Webmaster. Pictures and text are powerful on their own, but you can find those in any publication. Design and interactivity are what sets the Web apart. Like one of those old Choose Your Own Adventure books, you can use your design to guide viewers to links, which take them to new pages and give them a completely different experience from that of the next browser.

You can go wild with fonts.

You can make your photos burst into flames.

You can make little cartoon dudes dance across your page every five minutes.

You can layer your text onto a background of daisies or dolls or a picture of your dog.

Suffice to say, the options are limitless.

Here is the transformation of the goose logo. I am always trying to update the look of the site.

And, as in all things Webby, there are a number of different programs you can use to create your design. But I am loyal to Photoshop. In fact, all of Goosehead.com was designed with this program. Photoshop provides you with everything you need to graduate from a blank, white screen to a template to a vivid, throbbing Web page. And of course, it comes with a great tutorial to walk you through all its complexities.

You can download a trial version of Photoshop from Adobe.com, but you'll have to shell out some bucks for the actual program.

Trust me, Photoshop is worth every penny. Don't leave your hard drive without it.

Here is an early page of Goosehead.com.

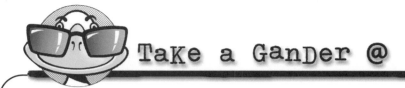

Here is an assortment of Photoshop sites that will help you navigate this fabulous tool . . .

Planet Photoshop: www.planetphotoshop.com
AdobePhotoshop: www.adobe.com/products/photoshop/main.html
Photoshop Café: www.photoshop-cafe.com
Deep Space Web: www.deepspaceweb.com

If you want to get acquainted with Flash, go to this cool site:
Flashzone: www.flashzone.com

Once you've stepped beyond your newbie phase, you might want to delve into the world of Java. If so, consult these great resources . . .

Gamelan: gamelan.earthweb.com: This is a great site for learning Java programming.
Javascripts: javascripts.com: I get a lot of scripts here that are free and allow me to use them.

ELATED: www.elated.com: Check out this all-in-one Web design resource for free buttons, bars, animated GIFs, bullets, backgrounds, clip art, and stock photos. And as if that weren't enough, they also offer Adobe Photoshop tips, Web design tips, Web page templates, and more.

Uh-oh! This is where the site started to look like every other teen site.

Goosehead is always under construction!

Goosehead.com
for teens that aren't
little Kids!

What? Why do they think they understand me...when they don't have a clue!

 Shopping   News  Goosehead Mail   Goose Gear  Movies • Music

How Goosehead came to be...

Bored, disgusted and wanting more!
È Click HereÇ

Books
È Want to check out some cool books, that I recommend. Click Here!

Parents • What should I do?
È Parentsoup   È Dating My Daughter, Click Here

Site Reviews
È Cyberteens
È Music Match Jukebox 3.1
È Qsound 3D Audio (Rate : 9.5/10)
È MP3 File Editor (Rate : 8/10)

Goosehead Editors
È Grab a Goosehead Banner
È Have something interesting to share?
È Become a Goosehead Editor

Quality Sites MP3
È MP3.com/index   È MP3 Hangout
È Free Stuff Centre   È MP3 Imperium
È MP3-2000   È MP3 Tip Europe
È MP3 Direct DI   È Request MP3
È Free and Legal   È Top Real Songs

Menu

Search Engines [for info on other stuff, that you can't find here]
Yahoo | AltaVista | Go.com | Excite | MSN | Lycos

Latest Songs Chart
MTV US Top20 | Billboard Top50

Chat [Come talk to us]
MP3 | VQF | MIDI | WAV

Advice
Drugs | Sex | Boyfriend | Girlfriend | Dating | Puberty | Ask Ashley | Misc

Leave a Message / Discussion Board

Goosehead Personal Page

Reference
Libraries | Dictionaries | Quotations...

Dating
Boner moves | How | Things | Embarresing Moments

Fashion
What's hot! | What's not! | This Months Featured Line | Buy it!

Celebs
Find 'em | The Hunks | The Babes

College
EliteSites | SAT | Scholarships

Free Things & Some Games

My Horoscope & The Joke Bloke

Art
Let's see it | Banned | You're kidding

Fitness
How to stay in Shape | Over-weight | I'm never gonna look like that | To hell with 'em

Only the best!

exclusive NEWS & REVIEWS from

 Search: [Popular Music ⬍]   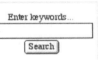 Enter keywords...

[   ]

[Search]

Buy your - Books • DVD's • Videos • CD's
All right here!

Then the site started to look like Yahoo.

119

Another Goosehead transition! I'm always changing.

The current Web page.

The Caveat . . .

The Caveat . . .

Okay, per your tutorial's instructions, you've built a nifty little Web page. It's humming along on your PC, and you can't wait to show it to the world.

Not so fast there!

Every Webmaster can cringingly remember building beautiful pages on their hard drives, then uploading them to the Web (as in the World Wide Web, where everybody and their brother can see it) only to realize that his or her site was filled with errors!

Murphy's law—the minute you go live, that's when you'll see a glaring mistake you've made.

Or you'll realize that some mysterious crack in the information highway has tripped up your page and filled it with nasty glitches.

Either way, you're humiliated.

To avoid this e-faux pas, always remember to test your page before uploading. The best way is to download both the Navigator and Explorer browsers, upload your Web site according to the instructions, and give it a whirl. You'll see the page up and humming just as it will when it goes live on the Web. And you'll be able to pinpoint and correct glitches away from the public's prying eyes.

Finding a Place to Roost . . . .

Finding a Place to Roost

Okay, now you're ready to come out of the closet with your very own Web site. How do you do it? You need to upload it onto an Internet server. As always on the Web, there are tons of options. You could try angelfire.com or geocities.com, but I most heartily recommend . . . Goosehead.com, of course!

First, you have to have a domain name, or a name for your Web site. My advice—come up with something unique but very simple. You want something catchy that people will remember, something that only takes a few keystrokes to type.

Once you've come up with the perfect moniker, you have to register it at a site like register.com. Follow the site's instructions—it's easy—and then pay up. It usually costs $35 per year.

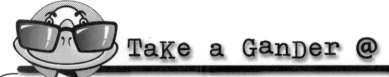

Take a Gander @

Here are a couple places you can go to register your domain name:
- *Network Solutions:* www.networksolutions.com
- *Register.com:* www.register.com

Then you go to your *Internet Service Provider*, otherwise known as an *ISP*, who will actually place your site on the Web. Your ISP will be your virtual host, usually for a fee of about $20 per month.

Warning: Your ISP might try to sell you your own server, at a much higher cost. But remember—you're a newbie. You so don't need your own server at this point in the game. So make sure you sign on with a virtual host.

You can create a free home page, but it's to your advantage to subscribe to your ISP's host machine because you'll be buying access to their services, like a *CGI-bin*. A *CGI* is an attachment that adds functionality to your site, enabling you, for instance, to create a message board. Some cost money, but it's usually easy to find a CGI that does what you need for free.

Another reason to sign on to a virtual host is for their technicians, who can walk you through their accessories and help you iron out ISP-unique glitches.

Take a GanDer @

SplitInfinity: **www.splitinfinity.com: This is my buddy Chris's site. He has a lot of great CGI scripts and they host Web sites.**

Live and on Computer . . .

Now that you have a host, you'll need a tool to actually put your pages onto the Web, or an FTP program. *FTP* stands for *File Transfer Protocol,* which basically means moving files from one place to another and vice versa. You can use your FTP to upload your site onto the Web and also to update it, change it, or remove it.

Though programs like GoLive have FTPs built into their programs, I prefer stand-alone ones like WS_FTP or Cute FTP. Recently I've been using Netload and Fetch, which is great for Macs.

The best part about these FTPs is they can all be downloaded for free from www.cnet.com. (This site, by the way, is also a source for many, many other cool programs. When you get there, be sure to browse around!)

Come on Down . . .

Your site is up and running on the World Wide Web! But, um, the only people who know this are you and your best friends.

So how do you get total strangers to check out your site? You hook up with search engines, so people know how to find your site.

There are a lot of services out there that say they'll submit your site to four hundred different search engines. This sounds sexy, but the reality is, most people only use about seven major search engines. I mean, when's the last time you went to UncleJoe's WebIndex? How about never. Glomming onto these fringe engines won't hurt you, but it probably won't get you a lot of hits, either.

What you want are the biggies: *Altavista, AOL, Deja News, Excite, Fast Search/All the Web, Google, HotBot, Infoseek, iWon, LookSmart, Lycos, MetaCrawler, MSN, Northern Light, WebCrawler, whatUseek, Snap, Yahoo*!

So how do these search engines work? You've been there as a browser. Say you type *teen, chat,* or *Ashley Power* into a search engine. Among your results, you are most likely going to discover Goosehead.com.

 Take a Gander @

Webmaster Expert: www.webmasterexpert.com: This site contains research and resources to make your hit counter explode and turn your Web site into an income stream.

So as a Webmaster, you need to attach key words to your site. The key words are stored in a device called a metatag—think of it as a sign that you'll use to get people's attention down when they're surfing.

Creating metatags is . . . well, it's a little complicated and more than you want to read about here. The best place to learn how to create one is in your editor manual. You can also check out the metatags on other Web sites by viewing their source code. If the site is similar to yours, check out the key words in their metatag and go ahead and filch some. Key words, after all, can't be copyrighted.

Take a GanDer @

Advanced Business Systems: www.scrubtheWeb.com/abs/meta-check.html:
This is a metatag builder and analyzer.

Metatags are supposed to have no more than twenty-one key words inside them. Of course, people cheat and use more words. It all depends on what theory you subscribe to.

All this means you should choose your key words wisely, placing them only once in the metatag but sprinkling them liberally (about three times) through your page, once in the page title and another time in the "alt tag" at the top of the page. Put more important key words near the front of the list in your metatag.

An Alternative Route . . . .

Let's face it. Not everybody is a DIY-type. That's why they invented speed-dial and Powerbars. And that's why I invented Goose village. I'm referring, of course, to the neighborhood in Goosehead.com

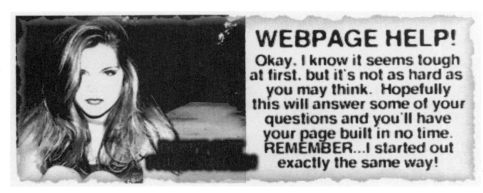

WEBPAGE HELP!
Okay. I know it seems tough at first, but it's not as hard as you may think. Hopefully this will answer some of your questions and you'll have your page built in no time. REMEMBER...I started out exactly the same way!

(www.goosehead.com/goosevillage/help/index.html) that can be a loving home to your Web site. What's more, Goosevillage has a step-by-step, hold-your-hand approach to setting up your new site.

How's it work? Read on. . .

Sign Up . . .

First things first, sign up for an account. Pick where you want your Web page to reside (i.e.; Gooseway, Gooseroad . . .). Make sure to remember what category you have picked to put your Web page in, because when you sign in to build your Web page it will ask you that. Now once you sign in, immediately go to the account information link and click on it. **(View graphic #1 below.)**

#1) NAME YOUR WEB SITE AND GIVE A SITE DESCRIPTION. This way it will show up in the directory. After you have named the site, hit the edit values button, then return to the home users preferences at the top left-hand corner link.

Okay, now it's time to build your page.

#1

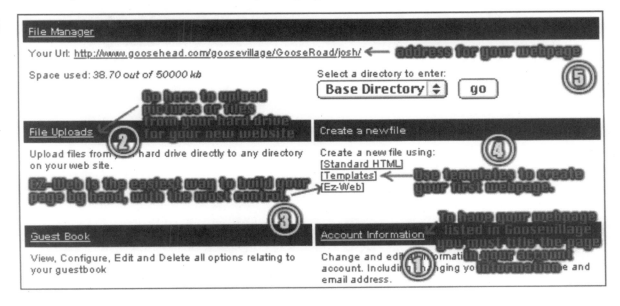

#2) Most everybody has some sort of image that they want on their Web page. Whether you downloaded something from the Web or you've scanned something, it's always nice to be able to put your own things onto your page. So, now you need to upload the file into a folder in your Web site. So, click on file uploads.

Now click on a browse button and find the .jpg or .gif file that you want to upload from your hard drive. Once you've placed the file into the box, either click "UPLOAD THESE FILES," or go to box number 2, and add another image. When you're ready, upload them. **(View graphic #2 below.)**

#2

Home :: File Uploads

Select up to 10 files at a time to upload from your computers hard drive to your web site.

click on the browse button and find the image you wish to use on your webpage that now resides on your harddrive.

Directory to upload files to: [Base Directory ▼]

1. [(example) myimage.gif] [Browse...]
2. [(example) dad.gif] [Browse...]
3. [(example) dog.gif] [Browse...]
4. [ ] [Browse...]
5. [ ] [Browse...]
6. [ ] [Browse...]
7. [ ] [Browse...]
8. [ ] [Browse...]
9. [ ] [Browse...]
10. [ ] [Browse...]

After you have choosen which files to upload, click below

[Upload these files]

Building Your Actual Pages . . .

Building Your Actual Pages . . .

Now that you have uploaded whatever graphics that you choose to use, the next step is actually building a page. Using the templates is an easy way to get started, **(View graphic #4 on next page)** and is worth playing around with just to get the hang of making a page. For this tutorial, click on the Ez-Web builder. **(View graphic #3 below.)**

#3

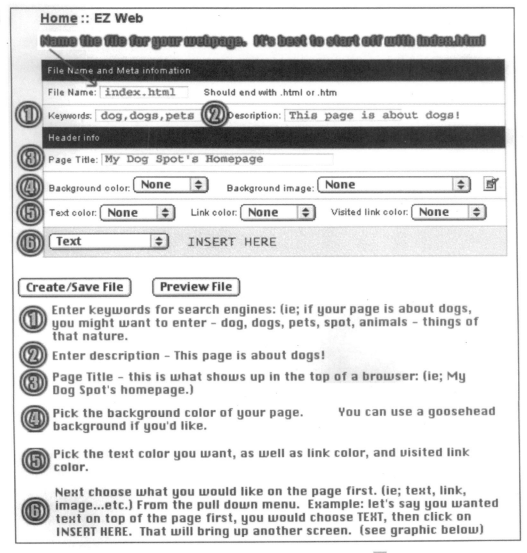

#4

Now Let's Say You Want to Add a Picture to Your Web Site . . . .

You would choose IMAGE from the pull-down menu, then click INSERT HERE. This will bring up another form that continues where you left off. Only now it will ask you for the image URL. **(View graphic #5 on next page.)**

#5

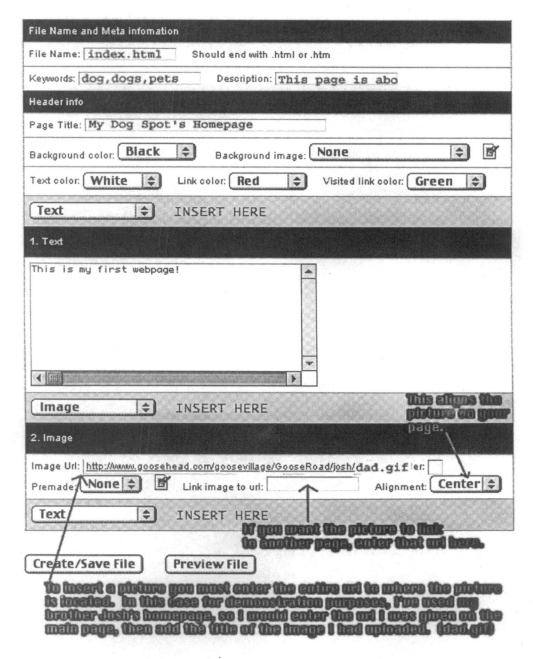

You're on Your Way . . .

You're on Your Way . . .

It's that simple. You can build other pages to link to after you've created your index page. And remember, it's okay to play and make mistakes, that's how you learn. You can always go back in and edit your page. PLAY and LEARN!

Where to Go When You're Stuck . . .

Where to Go When You're Stuck . . .

I've mentioned your tutorials, ISP technicians, and editor manuals that you can go to for troubleshooting. But remember, you should also feel free to access http://www.goosehead.com/started/index.html. Goosehead has an entire section devoted to nurturing teen Webmasters, answering your questions and steering you toward cool links offering everything from JavaScript games to CGI scripts.

Goosehead is also a great place to network with other Web heads, sharing ideas and chatting about your new HTML addiction! Believe me, you'll be hooked in no time.

Once that happens, make sure to e-mail me with your URL (your Web site address). I'm always on the lookout for the next hot new site. And it's entirely possible that that site will be yours!

TaKe a GanDer @

Here are some great general sites where you can find anything from Web design help to Java scripts to chats about your Web woes . . .

24 Fun.com: 24fun.com

EarthWeb: htmlgoodies.earthweb.com

When you need to check the hops, you need trace routes. Find them at:

Internet Access Inc. Traceroute: www.getnet.com/cgi-bin/trace

Macromedia: www.macromedia.com

Website Abstraction: wsabstract.com

PC Resources for Photoshop and the Digital Photographer: www.netins.net/showcase/wolf359/plugcomm.htm

Chapter Ten
You're in Business

So you've been futzing around with Adobe Photoshop for weeks and suddenly, you're a whiz! You've learned how to morph one photo into another. You've littered your template with schmancy backgrounds and giggly cartoons. You've got links galore.

But have you got anything to say?

Oh . . .

Forgot about that part, did ya'?

Designing your site, with all its uploading, downloading, chatting, and Webcamming can be pretty glamorous. But somewhere along the way, a lot of folks forget the most important feature on any Web site—content.

Without a fabulous idea, some rocking words, or some scintillating snaps, your Web site is going to be little more than an E-scrapbook, i.e., not very interesting to anyone besides you and your buds.

There's nothing wrong with that. But if you want to create a Goosehead—a destination that attracts a steady and increasing number of hits, not to mention investors and advertisers—you're going to have to get busy filling your pages with unique, sustainable stuff.

Take a Gander @

When seeking fodder to fill your site, check out these hot links . . .

isyndicate: www.isyndicate.com: Go here for content as well as info that can help make your site better.

Mac.org: www.mac.org: Apple addict? Find great downloads here.

CNET Download for Macs and PC's: download.cnet.com/downloads: This is a great place to get some free downloads and shareware stuff to use.

Wrong Warez: www.geocities.com/web_warez: In addition to a bunch of apps you can download, Wrong Warez features great games.

The Big Idea . . .

Where to begin?

Some folks are lucky enough to come to the Web simply looking for an outlet for their idea—a place to sell a screenplay, post poetry, place a mega–personal ad, or run a serial comic strip.

Others are so psyched about the medium, they simply want to be a part of it, but they have no idea how.

For those of you in the latter camp, the place to start is the Web itself. It's time to grab your mouse and get surfing.

That's how I came up with the notion for Goosehead.com. I was looking for a teen site that met all my needs—a place with cool chats, with no grown-ups, without in-your-face marketing scams, and without a girls-only vibe. When I couldn't find such a thing, I realized I should create it myself. And thus, Goosehead.com was born.

Or perhaps you'll see a site, say a movie freak destination like ain't-it-cool-news.com or a hip reader like Salon.com and say, "I can do something like this with a twist." Or, "I can do this much better." Or, "I can do this for teens or African Americans or the multipierced!" My point is—don't be afraid to tread in the same territory that others have explored first. The reason you see a Caribou Coffee across the street from a Starbuck's is that people like choice. There's nothing wrong with giving them one more bean to choose from.

The World Wide Web is so enormous, it's almost impossible to create a Web site that's 100 percent unique. I mean, Goosehead is one of hundreds of teen sites. It's just the only one with Ashley Power's spin on it.

On the other hand, you don't want to create an evil clone. Nothing would suck more than slaving for months on your quirky brainchild, craftswithnoodles.com, only to discover that some other pasta impresario has beat you to the punch with his almost identical noodlecrafts.com.

Summation? Your job isn't to come up with an idea that's never been done or to replicate the same old same-old. You simply have to tackle your idea with a new angle, a personal twist, a fresh character, or some cool new format.

One way to stay cutting edge is to keep up with new technology. It seems like every time you turn around, there's Flash's cool younger brother or HTML's heir popping up on the Internet horizon. MP3 technology, new Webcams, scanners, digital film processors, memory sticks—you name it, it's in development as I write this. To keep your site as hip as possible, I suggest you access every new gizmo, graphic, application, or design tool you can. This will draw techheads looking for examples of the next new thing, as well as graphics snobs who will only visit the most dazzling sites on the Web.

Shoot, Aim, Shoot Again

Shoot, Aim, Shoot Again

That's our motto at Goosehead.com. What does it mean? Don't hold back! If you've got an idea, go with it! Experiment! Toss it out there. Is it odd? Is it off-the-wall? So much the better.

Nobody ever got labeled a visionary by being timid.

That said, I should point out another phrase often bandied about our offices: remember your audience.

For us, that means crazy ideas are great, as long as they're tailored to teens. A rock-the-vote feature, for instance, while noble and even cool, would miss the mark for much of Goosehead's under-eighteen audience. We also have to make sure to be gender inclusive. Just because I, as the girl CEO of Goosehead, might want makeup tips on the home page (not that I do!!!) doesn't mean that's the best choice for my audience, which is about half male.

So yeah—take those risks, have a blast. But be careful not to alienate your audience when you do, whether they be teens of all stripes like Goosehead viewers, Latin Americans, dog owners, grass mowers, or chocoholics.

How do you know if you're hitting the mark? Solicit feedback in a big way. Beg your viewers to attend chats, to post their opinions on your message boards, and to e-mail you like crazy. Then listen! And be open to making changes that satisfy your viewers' demands.

Of course, you can't please everybody all of the time. I learned that when we started scattering my photos throughout Goosehead. Our advisers had convinced me that this would be a good marketing tool; that it would make Goosehead stand apart from a host of other teen sites. And they were right—our character-driven site generated a lot of press and tons of hits.

But my photos also created some dissension among Goosehead's ranks. Many of the female viewers (myself included!) got sick of seeing Ashley Power all over the place.

But when we thinned the photos out, a lot of guy viewers complained. (*What-EVER!*)

As a compromise, we moved many of the pics to a photo gallery. It lowered the Ash-saturation of the site, but didn't remove the images entirely.

I'm not saying you should be a slave to your viewers' whims. At the end of the day, it's still your voice and your name on your site, so you have to believe in what it says. But when there are so many options on the Internet, ignoring your viewers' feedback could mean sudden death. It could also mean missing out on some great ideas.

Again, look at Goosehead. One of our best features—Stephanie Joy Pruner's column—started with the e-mail she sent the site, a witty rant about our shortcomings. I could have tossed out her comments simply because they were negative or because I might not have agreed with them. Instead, I took Stephanie's comments to heart—and offered her a job. And I believe Goosehead is better for it.

Then again, maybe not. Tell me what you think. I promise to listen!

Know Yourself, Know Your Web Page

Your audience isn't the only factor you have to worry about when creating content. You also have to keep your eye on the prize—that is, your mission.

Say you start a Web site that reviews MP3s. There are so many directions in which you could take this idea. You could have a place on your site to download new tunes, a chat and message board about new MP3s, rock-star interviews, a place to create your own audio samples . . .

Then suppose you decide to create a little diversion on your site, a page devoted to your other passion—chameleons.

Here's your result—a lot of dazed, confused, and even perturbed surfers.

"Why?" you ask. "I'm way into MP3s and chameleons. And it is a separate page."

Here's the prob. Your Web site's tangent may start with chameleons. But then you may branch into a fave ice-cream flavor poll or an online SAT support group. Next thing you know, you're doing that sticky-film strip-poker thing.

And your site starts to resemble a schizophrenic octopus with too many legs, each jerking in a different direction. In other words, it's a big mess. What's more, your original concept—MP3s—is bound to get lost in the shuffle.

One secret to a fab Web site is focus. Look at something like theknot.com. This Web site is all about weddings. It has a million different pages and features, but they all, in some way, pertain to weddings. Goosehead.com follows the same rule. While we have dozens of pages, from games to documentaries to homework help, every bit of our site is made for and by teens.

Not only will staying focused give your site a solid identity, it'll also keep you from getting overwhelmed. Want to see viewers drop you faster than a blind date with B.O.? Then launch a Web page that veers out of control—that crashes all the time because you couldn't handle all your page links; that's too big and unwieldy to make for easy navigation; that features so many pages you never have time to update any of them.

Keep your mission in control and, as Dr. Seuss says, "Oh, the places you'll go!"

Taking Care of Business . . .

Once your site is really humming along, you might want to do what I did with Goosehead and take it to the next level—form a company, hire employees, get advertisers and investors, and maybe even score some profits some day.

There are a million ways to go about this huge task and the methods are changing every day. I won't offer step-by-step rules to creating your own business because the first rule would be, well, there are no rules.

But here are some tips . . .

Gather Round Ye Cheerleaders . . .

No Webmaster is an island, especially if she's a CEO. The first thing Mark and I did when I decided to expand Goosehead is seek investors.

Actually, the very first thing we did was project our expenses. We considered everything we would need for my vision, including a budget for *Whatever*, money to pay for office space and employees, money for office supplies, and so on and so on and so on.

When we made our budget, we tossed out the conventional business

Working out the budget is tough, but necessary.

model called 80/20. This is the idea that you commit 80 percent of your budget to marketing and advertising and 20 percent to content. Now, 80/20 is based on the notion that, without advertising and marketing, no one will ever see your content. But we're talking about the Web, where word of mouth can create overnight sensation. And my very media-savvy parents also knew that no amount of expensive advertising could compete with cost-free coverage in the media. So we decided that our advertising would consist of little more than press packets to be sent to magazines, TV stations, and newspapers. The cost? Minimal—which meant almost all of our budget could be devoted to content. And that meant that we could propose a budget much smaller than that of the average start-up.

But who did we propose this budget to? Those potential investors—people who would contribute funds or services to Goosehead with the understanding that, should the site make money some day, they would receive a piece of the pie.

Since I'd already been e-corresponding with a bunch of Webmasters and other experts, Mark and I invited them to a meeting in Las Vegas. We all gathered around a hotel conference-room table and I told these folks about my ideas. I proposed *Whatever*, a venture that was going to require some serious cash. I laid out my future plans for the site. Mark and I explained every facet of our financial plan.

And our friends were convinced. We walked out of that hotel with partners. We documented what each person would contribute to the company and worked out what percentage of the profits they would someday get. We didn't use lawyers to draw up complicated contracts—we simply created our own, mutually satisfactory documents. That way we didn't have to shell out thousands in lawyers' fees.

This was one of the many ways in which we at Goosehead started out with our belts tightened.

How I Hooked Up with an Oscar-Nominated Actor . . .

In 2000, Goosehead.com found a new partner—Richard Dreyfuss. I know what some viewers must have thought when I made the announcement on the site: Here's a silver-haired serious actor and here's an edgy, teen Web site. What a random connection!

Maybe it is, but if you ask me, that's the beauty of it. When you're in business, you have to be open to even the most unusual or unlikely opportunities.

Our association with Richard came through his family. Richard's brother, Lorin, is my mother's business partner at her advertising agency. And Lorin's daughter—Natalie—plays Skye's little sister on *Whatever*.

When Richard checked out our show on Goosehead.com, he saw something that excited him, a cool use of this new, online medium. And he wanted to get involved.

Random or not, I was all for it. Especially when Richard and I started meeting and discussing creative ideas for the site. We were totally in sync and equally enthusiastic. Both of us agreed that we wanted to keep the content edgy and designed specifically for teens.

Together we decided that Richard would help bring new original shows to Goosehead, to ride *Whatever*'s popularity wave. Since then, he's been a crucial adviser on all Goosehead TV developments.

Richard's experiences as a father of teenagers makes him even more excited about designing content and programming that will appeal to teens. The guy is far from clueless. So, while I still give all our ideas my teen seal of approval, his creative notions have been totally key.

Can you imagine what Goosehead would have missed out on had I rejected this alliance, just because it was random? Open-mindedness to brilliant folks like Richard is one thing that's made Goosehead.com a site to be reckoned with.

AshLey and new Partner Richard Dreyfuss

You with the Stars in Your Eyes . . .

Just between you and me—greed and impatience cause the downfall of a lot of Internet start-ups. Folks hear about a twenty-five-year-old dot.com millionaire and think, "That could so be me!"

But here's the truth about a lot of those dot.com richies. Before they made it big, they toiled on their sites in poverty and obscurity. For years. Only after suffering and starving for a long time did they turn a profit or sell to a big corporation for major bucks.

Here's what happens if you start out with dollar signs in your eyes. You make up a million-dollar budget. You call up your best friends and say, "I'll be president, you be vice president, you be the chief financial officer, and each of us will make a salary of $100,000." And then, after a few months of the lux life, you find yourself broke and at the end of your rope, along with hundreds of other stunned former e-entrepreneurs.

Here's what we did at Goosehead. We paid our people . . . nothing. That's right. We found people who were passionate about my idea and had the patience to work for free in the hopes that someday, the site would pay off.

Hiring teenagers was especially easy. After all, they don't have to pay their own rent or bills. In the case of adults, we hired people with other sources of income. My mother, for instance, owns an advertising agency and contributes whatever extra time she can to Goosehead. Our partner Pat Galvin has stakes in several Web sites, so all his eggs are not in Goosehead's basket.

We also run a very tight ship in our office. Even though I'm the CEO, I share an office. So does most of our staff. Our space is comfortable but sparse—no cappuccino machines or fancy furniture, thank you. We're talking IKEA all the way.

Has this tightfistedness paid off? Well, Goosehead is still here. And as dot.coms die with each passing day, that's a major accomplishment.

 Say Cheese!

One of the ways Goosehead got so big was through press attention. And how did we get so much attention? I have to admit it—sheer luck.

It started with one newspaper reporter discovering the site. Did he get excited about my bitchin' graphics and stellar pages? My impressive hit parade? My inspired content?

No. He honed in on me—a fourteen-year-old girl CEO. His article was mostly about me, how I started Goosehead and the odd fact that I am boss to, among other folks, my own parents.

Dozens of articles and TV spots later, my story is still Goosehead's story. My photograph is still Goosehead's image.

Is this the path I would have chosen? Not really. Anyone who's been to Goosehead knows that it's not "The Ashley Power Show." It's filled with the voices of columnists, viewers, contributors, and the ensemble cast of *Whatever*.

But when the press decided to hone in on me, there was nothing I could do about it (short of refusing interviews). And the bottom line was, these articles made Goosehead famous, which increased its hits, which brought more advertisers, alliances, and contributors to the site. It made MGM's Hank Cohen take notice and offer us a TV production deal. It enabled Goosehead to grow even bigger and brighter.

Be savvy about your business plan.

Stay Flexible . . .

Stay Flexible . . .

Of course, none of Goosehead's success would have happened if we had wrung our hands and said, "This is not going according to plan!"

The first rule of Internet business (or any business, come to think of it) is to stay flexible. Make a calendar, make a budget, make an outline—and then be willing to go in a completely different direction if the wind changes.

When the publicity storm made Goosehead a hot commodity about a year earlier than we'd planned for, we had to skip ahead in our outline and adapt, adapt, adapt.

Is this process messy? Yes. Is it also fun? Yes! Staying on your toes like this is also the only way to survive.

Embrace the Competition . . .

Embrace the Competition . . . .

You know that saying, "If you can't beat 'em, join 'em?" It should be on the ten commandments of doing business on the Internet. After word of mouth and media attention, one of the best ways for Web browsers to find you is through other Web sites.

That's why, against all appearances otherwise, it pays to sleep with the enemy.

For instance, Alloy.com, a mega teen Web site, came to Goosehead to form an alliance. They saw that we had something to offer their readers and installed a Goosehead hot link on their site.

This looks like Alloy is sending viewers away! But actually, they're keeping fans loyal by giving them plenty of options, even if it means farming them out to other Web sites.

So, instead of floating solo, make sure you form strategic alliances with your Web brethren. Perhaps it'll delay your ascension to the Internet's number-one spot. On the other hand, without these relationships, you'll never even get a peek at that peak.

If You Believe . . .

Okay, here's my most important advice for making your Web site white-hot. When all is said and done, all you need is passion for your creation, confidence in yourself, and the ability to ignore the naysayers.

I guarantee, when you get your Web site rolling, grown-ups will come out of the woodwork, harrumphing, "You want to run your own Web company? But you're only thirteen!"

Whereupon you can say, "So what? Lemme tell you about this girl named Ashley Power . . ."

Good luck, e-friends. Catch you on the www.

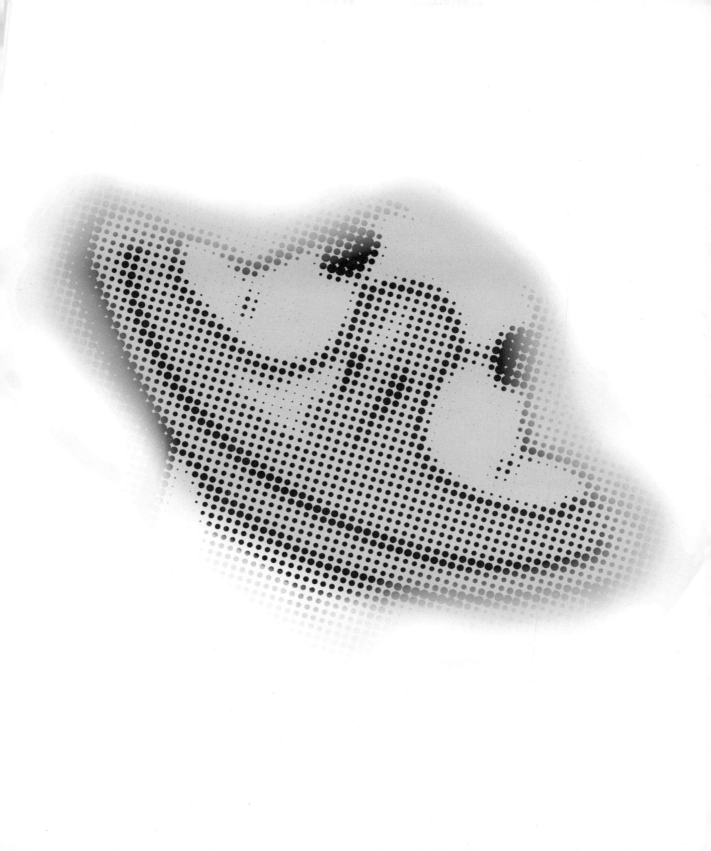

Acknowledgments

- **Mom** and **Mark**—my partners in crime
- **Josh, Dad, Grandma** (keep the gossip coming!), **Whit, Zac, Elliot, Calvin, Isabel, Melanie**
- **Nina, Pat, Lori, Nick, Trevor, Hallie**—Thanks to all for putting up with me and teaching me the business.
- **Mel McKeon** and **Laura Myones**
- **Matt Rice** and **Broderkurland, Puma. Monson, Richard Dreyfuss, Lorin Dreyfuss, Barnes Morris, Klein and Yorn, David Adelman, Lisa Kastel** and **Kristin Malaby, Andrew Winter**
- **Mike Badami** (thanks for believing!)
- **Sean** and **Tommy**—Thanks so much!!
- **3:33: Tom, Jason, Ted, Tom Shadyac**
- **Killing Heidi!** Love you **Ella, Jes, Adam**, and **Waz**
- **TJ**—always . . . "Don't take the girl. . . ."
- **Arelyn, Kris, Britt, Meg, Ryan, Ashlee, Marce** . . . I could go on forever!
- **Elizabeth Lenhard** and **Helen Perelman**—Thanks so much! Without you this book would have NEVER been finished! Much love!
- **Emily Lo**, thank you for all your work.
- **Karen Hudson**, the design looks GREAT!
- To all those I may have not mentioned, you know who you are and you have a special place in my life!
- **To my Goosehead family**, all my friends on the boards, to my late-night chatters . . . thank you! Couldn't have done it without you!

Notes

Notes

Notes

Notes

Notes